CURTAINS

Tom Mallin is a remarkable 'na[...] early forties, who was totally un[...] first novel Dodecahedron was pu[...] and Curtains was produced at the Traverse Theatre Club, Edinburgh. The film rights of Dodecahedron were bought within ten days of publication, after it had received great praise from the critics - and since then Mr. Mallin has not looked back.

Curtains, his first play to be performed and published, is a terrifyingly acute and chilling study of a three-handed relationship between a man, his wife and a woman he picks up. The conflicts between the three of them, the cold-blooded sexual permutations they play and their sheer nastiness and vindictiveness, leading to a horrifyingly gruesome climax, are grippingly presented in a clinically naturalistic manner: yet their spite and brutality are always credibly rooted in their frustrations and are never displayed for purely sensational effect. In its total impact, it conveys brilliantly how an unhappy marriage can release all the most destructive qualities in its participants and as such is in many ways reminiscent of Edward Albee's Who's Afraid of Virginia Woolf?, though it has a style all of its own. Its first production, at the Tower Theatre, Canonbury, London, in January, 1970, received praise from The Guardian: later in the year, it received a much-acclaimed first professional production at The Traverse Theatre Club, Edinburgh, as part of the 1970 Edinburgh Festival, and this production was seen at The Open Space Theatre, London, in early 1971.

Tom Mallin has since written four more plays, and another novel, Knut, which will be published by Allison & Busby in 1971. He lives in Suffolk with his American-born wife and two sons.

PLAYSCRIPT 57
'curtains'

tom mallin

CALDER AND BOYARS · LONDON

First published in Great Britain 1971 by
Calder and Boyars Limited
18 Brewer Street, London wl

All performing rights in the play
are strictly reserved and applications
for performances should be made to
BKM (Personal Agency) Ltd
27 Curzon Street London Wl

No performance of the play
may be given unless a licence has
been obtained prior to rehearsal

ISBN 0 7145 0792 X Cloth Edition
ISBN 0 7145 0793 8 Paper Edition

Printed by photo-lithography
and made in Great Britain at
The Pitman Press, Bath.

CURTAINS

CURTAINS was first performed by The Tavistock Repertory
Company at The Tower Theatre, Canonbury, London, on
9th January, 1970, with the following cast:

NIALL SCRINGEOUR	Colin Ley
MILDRED WRINGE	Patricia Gerrard
GLADYS SPENDLOVE	Joanne Harding

The play was directed by Richard Penny.

CURTAINS was first performed as a professional
production at The Traverse Theatre Club, Edinburgh, on
9th July, 1970, with the following cast:

NIALL SCRINGEOUR	Nigel Hawthorne
MILDRED WRINGE	Antonia Pemberton
GLADYS SPENDLOVE	Ursula Smith

The play was directed by Michael Rudman.

ACT ONE

Scene One

(The room one Sunday morning.

MILDRED, lying unmoving on the bed, is hidden
beneath the disordered bedclothes. From the
bathroom there comes the sound of water swilling
away down a waste pipe. When the bathroom door is
pushed open, NIALL, clad only in his underpants,
enters drying his hair vigorously on a towel. Having
dried his hair, NIALL throws the towel on to the bed,
walks to the upright, wooden chair and sorts through
his discarded clothing. Unable to find what he is
looking for, he flings down the clothes with a gesture
of irritation and, going to the wardrobe, rummages
about, letting fall whatever he discards. Finding a
vest he worms his way into it. After choosing a shirt
and a clean pair of socks, he sits on the bed.
MILDRED stirs, sniffs and clears her throat. NIALL
glances at her covered form, sighs deeply and draws
on his socks. Still seated, he puts on the crumpled
shirt and buttons himself into it. Dragging a pair of
wrinkled trousers off the chair, he puts his feet into
them, stands, tucks in his shirt, and, while having
difficulty closing up the zip, wriggles his feet into a
pair of shoes. Going back to the wardrobe, he con-
jures from the disorder a fistful of ties. He takes a
long time to decide which one to wear. Choosing a
red one, he throws the rest of the ties back into the

7

wardrobe and goes and stands before the mirror)

MILDRED. (from under the blankets) What time is it?
(NIALL glances at the bed and then back at his dusty
image in the mirror) WHAT'S THE TIME? (NIALL
pulls his tie undone with a gesture of irritation and,
walking to the window, parts the curtains and stands
looking down into the street. MILDRED pokes her
head out from beneath the bedclothes) WHAT YOU
DOING?

NIALL. (turning to her) You asked me the time.

(MILDRED grunts and disappears under the blankets)

Do you want to know?

MILDRED. I asked, didn't I?

NIALL. It isn't early. The milkman's already dotted the
steps with bottles. And it isn't late because hardly
anyone's took them in yet. Perhaps it's Sunday.
(then, with relish) SUNDAY! (and he rubs his hands
together)

MILDRED. (still entombed) Is it Sunday?

NIALL. Most of the curtains are still drawn. It could
be Sunday. Or d-o-o-m-s-d-a-y.

MILDRED. It's very quiet.

NIALL. The road has been layered with straw.

MILDRED. (her head above the bedclothes) The
council's covered the street with straw?

NIALL. To dampen the crunch of the iron wheels on the
grit and to muffle the clatter of the horse's hooves.

MILDRED. The milkman's got an electric van now - with
soft rubber tyres.

8

NIALL. So the corpse can be drawn slowly and silently into the wastes of the cemetery - that's why the straw's been laid.

MILDRED. You fibber.

NIALL. The lamp posts are strung about with crepe - like black maypoles - for a dance of death.

MILDRED. It's not true about the straw - is it?

NIALL. I am the one looking out of the window.

MILDRED. But there's no straw.

NIALL. Come and see for yourself.

MILDRED. You're not going to trick me into exposing myself at the window.

NIALL. No. You'd only see the pavements and the unswept road.

MILDRED. I didn't imagine for one moment that the Council would cover the street with straw. I thought you were lying. You were lying - weren't you?

NIALL. I lie to comfort myself.

MILDRED. (lying back) It was the sound of feet which woke me.

NIALL. I tip-toe through your life, my dear. Living my death.

MILDRED. It must have been the Catholics hurrying to their early Mass.

NIALL. It wasn't the creak of their bending knees which stirred your sleep. It was the dirt of my earthly body swilling down the drain.

MILDRED. God knows - they've sins enough to atone for.

NIALL. I am guilty of innocence father...

MILDRED. This road should be renamed O'Connell Street...

NIALL. ... and yet... I have holy stoned myself to a sabbatical whiteness... (he turns to MILDRED)... just for you.

MILDRED. ... then you and the Irish could pig-in together.

NIALL. Yes Father.

(Silence)

MILDRED. (propping herself up on one elbow and listening) It's as quiet as the tomb outside.

NIALL. I told you - it's the reverend hush of mourning.

MILDRED. Even the birds are silent.

NIALL. It's ominous.

MILDRED. Oppressive. And so still. Listen. Not a sound.

NIALL. Man respects the dead, but despises the living - and both in silence.

MILDRED. I wouldn't be surprised if it didn't storm. There's thunder in the air.

NIALL. And the smell of rotting corpses.

(There is a sound)

MILDRED. What was that? Was that thunder?

NIALL. No. Flies. The angry buzz of flies converging

10

on the same damp fold of flesh to lay their eggs.

MILDRED. Don't be so silly. Flies don't come out in the winter time.

NIALL. They are burrowing into the dead.

MILDRED. Has someone died?

NIALL. Everyone in the street is dead.

MILDRED. Idiot. (and she lays back)

NIALL. Only I am alive. The rest of you are dead.

MILDRED. They'd come running soon enough if you dared to lay a finger on me.

NIALL. I've never fingered a corpse.

MILDRED. As likely as not they're still all sleeping. It IS Sunday, remember.

NIALL. Have I?

MILDRED. They're still in bed.

NIALL. Yes. But dead. That's why all the curtains are drawn and the milk has been delivered in black bottles.

MILDRED. Now I know you're lying.

NIALL. (turning from the window) Is your explanation any better?

MILDRED. You said it was early.

NIALL. No one sleeps this late - even on a Sunday. (walking towards the mirror) Perhaps they sense the spring stirring their sluggish blood.

MILDRED. In that case they'd all be up and doing.

11

NIALL. Enjoying each other's flesh.

MILDRED. Opening windows and shaking out their mops; filling the air with dust and plumping eider-downs.

NIALL. (sniffing) I can already detect in the slight breeze the unmistakeable scent of sperm...

MILDRED. Or banging their doormats against... WHAT DID YOU SAY?

NIALL. I said they must be up to something.

MILDRED. Like what, for instance?

NIALL. What most people do. On Sunday mornings. In bed. Excepting us.

MILDRED. (sitting up suddenly) PIG!

NIALL. Yes! Yes, I'm a pig. Pink and hairless. Always snuffling and rooting in my own dung and ready to mount my sow if only she'd turn her great haunches into the wind. You're right - I'm a pig.

(NIALL turns his back on her and tries to tie his tie whilst looking in the mirror. MILDRED swings her feet out of bed and sits on the edge, dazed. Seeing the curtains partly open, she gets off the bed, muttering)

NIALL. Goodmorning. Goodmorninggoodmorninggood- morning.

MILDRED. (as she closes the curtains hurriedly) You know I don't like having·the curtains open.

(NIALL raises his eyebrows, takes a deep breath, and tries to concentrate on the problem of tying his tie. MILDRED slops into the bathroom)

YOU ROTTEN SWINE!

NIALL. (to his image in the mirror) Grunt you pig.
Grunt.

MILDRED. (appearing at the open bathroom door) YOU'VE
LET ALL THE BATHWATER OUT!

NIALL. (having difficulties with his tie) Grunts.

MILDRED. WHY?

NIALL. (undoing the knot in his tie and starting all over
again) It was MY bathwater.

MILDRED. You did it on purpose.

NIALL. There's plenty of hot water left.

MILDRED. That's not the point. You know I only like
bathing in your bathwater.

NIALL. (dissatisfied with the knot he has tied) DAMN!
(he wrenches his tie off and turns) From now on,
you fill your own bath! The water I bathe in is
MINE! Do you understand? MINE! AND I CAN DO
WHAT I LIKE WITH IT!

MILDRED. (throwing herself on to the bed) You can
drown in it for all I care! (she shrugs up the bedclothes and is lost from view) PIG!

NIALL. Men drown their sorrows in beer - not in bathwater! Idiot.

(He looks in the mirror and begins to reknot his
tie. Unable to see in the darkened room, he turns on
the light. After looking in the mirror he is still
dissatisfied so he strides up to the window and opens
the curtains wide. MILDRED sits bolt upright,
flinging the bedclothes from her)

MILDRED. Have you gone MAD! What d'you think
you're doing?

NIALL. I'm trying to tie my tie. I CAN'T SEE!

MILDRED. Turn the light on then, you fool.

NIALL. It IS turned on!

MILDRED. (struggling off the soft bed, runs to the window) I'm not having them open. (she tugs the curtains closed)

NIALL. I WANT THEM OPEN!

(As MILDRED turns to scramble back into bed, NIALL swishes them apart)

AND THEY'RE STAYING OPEN!

MILDRED. (turning and springing) OH NO, THEY'RE NOT!

(She snatches them together. NIALL opens them again. Shouting, they struggle with the curtains and with each other. Suddenly the pole on which the curtains hang springs from the wall and falls. NIALL and MILDRED are enveloped by the curtains. Shrieking, MILDRED frees herself and collapses on the bed, weeping hysterically. Drawing the curtains off his head, NIALL stands looking round the brilliantly lit room. For the first time the extreme shabbiness of the room is revealed. Through the window can be seen the roofs and windows of the houses opposite. To NIALL the room is suddenly grotesque, almost obscene. He lays the pole on the floor and, picking his way carefully and slowly, he walks to the bed and leans over MILDRED)

NIALL. I'm sorry, love. Truly. (MILDRED shrugs off his comforting arm) But I am. I wouldn't have had it happen for the world. Honestly. (MILDRED allows him to smooth her hair) Come on. You get back into bed. (hiding her face from the light, MILDRED curls up and NIALL covers her with the bedclothes) There's my girl. You stay there.

Comfy?

MILDRED. Do something quickly, Niall. Please.

NIALL. Yes, all right. I'll put them back up again.
Just you stay curled up tight. I'll soon have them
fixed. Close your eyes.

(Turning away from the bed, NIALL tips the clothes
from the wooden chair and carries it to the window.
After much manoeuvring, he manages to mount the
chair with the pole and curtains in such a way that it
is not difficult for him to rehang them. He steps
down and regards his handiwork with satisfaction)

There. All done.

(Silence)

(MILDRED slowly emerges from beneath the bedclothes)

See? Now. What about getting up?

MILDRED. NO. (she disappears under the bedclothes
again. NIALL sighs and goes back to the mirror to
tie his tie. After several attempts he loses his
patience, rips the tie off and flings it from him,
cursing)

(from under the bedclothes) What you doing?

NIALL. I was trying to tie my damned tie. That's what!

MILDRED. (as she sits up) Oh for goodness sake let me
do it for you. Where is it?

(NIALL looks for his tie, finds it, picks it up and
goes to the bed. Sheepishly, he holds the tie out to
MILDRED who takes it from him. They look at each
other)

Well, I'm not going to stand up!

(She swings her legs out of bed and sits on the edge.
NIALL bends forward)

I can't do it like that. You'll have to kneel.

(NIALL stands erect and looks down at MILDRED)

Well, do you want me to do it or don't you?

NIALL. Yes. Please.

MILDRED. Then kneel.

(Silence)

THERE.

(She points to the floor between her feet)

KNEEL.

(Slowly, obediently, NIALL sinks to his knees
between MILDRED's parted thighs and looks into
her eyes)

And behave yourself.

NIALL. (weakly) Yes.

(MILDRED ties the knot in his tie swiftly and
expertly, draws it tight and adjusts the points of
NIALL's wrinkled collar; smoothing and pressing
them down)

MILDRED. There.

(She leans back and they regard each other in silence.
Suddenly NIALL buries his face in MILDRED's lap
and slides his arms about her)

NIALL. It's been such a long time. Such a long, long
time.

16

MILDRED. You promised to be good. Didn't you?

(Silence. Then, almost tenderly, MILDRED leans over NIALL and puts her arms about him)

Would you do something for me?

(NIALL nods)

Anything?

NIALL. (looking up into her face) Whatever you want.

MILDRED. Promise?

(NIALL, after a moment's hesitation, nods)

Will you tack the curtains down?

NIALL. (taken aback) Tack what?

MILDRED. The curtains. I want you to nail them down. So they won't open. (and, as an afterthought:) They wouldn't fall down then. Would they?

NIALL. (laying his hands on MILDRED's thighs) Mildred dear. (he removes his right hand and places it over his heart) I will never open them again unless you ask me. I promise. I won't ever TOUCH them.

MILDRED. (brushing away NIALL's hand from her thigh) You said you'd do anything I asked.

NIALL. Yes. But I didn't expect...

MILDRED. (pushing NIALL over) I'll do it myself then. (standing and stepping over him) Where do you keep the tacks and hammer?

NIALL. (scrambling to his feet) YOU CAN'T GO NAILING DOWN CURTAINS!

MILDRED. Out of my way. (pushing NIALL) Where are

they?

NIALL. Where are what?

MILDRED. THE TACKS AND THE HAMMER. WHERE
HAVE YOU HIDDEN THEM?

NIALL. I haven't hidden them!

MILDRED. But you know where they are.

NIALL. I'm not saying.

MILDRED. Niall, I want them. If necessary I'll turn
this place inside out 'til I find them. WHERE ARE
THEY?

NIALL. You're cold.

MILDRED. It shouldn't be too difficult to find them. (she
goes towards the wardrobe)

NIALL. You're getting warmer.

MILDRED. (pulling everything out of the wardrobe and
throwing them on the floor) You can't hide things
from me.

NIALL. Colder.

MILDRED. (in desperation) Damn and blast you! Where
are they?

NIALL. (as MILDRED disappears into the bathroom)
Cold. Much colder. F-r-e-e-z-i-n-g.

(From the bathroom comes the sound of things
being shifted about. A bottle breaks and MILDRED
storms back into the room, puffing away the loose
hair which has fallen into her eyes. Exasperated,
she runs her fingers through her hair and points at
NIALL)

MILDRED. I'll find them. I'LL SPEND ALL DAY

18

LOOKING!

NIALL. Warmer.

MILDRED. (as she goes into the kitchen) I'll make you
suffer for this...

(From the kitchen comes the sound of pots and
crockery being roughly handled and the sounds of
cupboard doors being opened and banged shut. An
avalanche of cutlery showers on to the floor and
MILDRED is heard cursing. When she returns she
is trembling)

And to think I tied your bloody tie for you!

NIALL. Damn the tie! (he tears it off and throws it on
to the floor)

MILDRED. (already sweeping the clothes off the back
of the armchair) And DAMN you! (she tilts up the
armchair and looks underneath. The chair topples
over) Pig. PIG!

(NIALL grunts and pulls a face)

I've had just about as much as I can stand from you.

(She opens the lid of the trunk and all the crockery
slides off it, breaking. On her hands and knees, she
rummages in the trunk, flinging out odds and ends)

I don't know how I've put up with you all this time.
You and your dirty habits. WHERE ARE THEY?

(She flings a garment back into the trunk and sits
back on her haunches)

Damn you Niall. I WANT THOSE TACKS AND THE
HAMMER. WHERE ARE THEY?

(Silence)

THE BED! Of course.

(MILDRED crawls on all fours to the bed and feels about underneath it, withdrawing miscellaneous clothes, books, odd shoes, etc. all covered thick in dust. Lying on her stomach she peers under the bed)

Hello, what's this?

(She struggles out a wooden chest painted bright red. NIALL takes out a wooden chest painted bright red. NIALL takes a step forward, he looks anxious. MILDRED settles back on her haunches)

Who said I wouldn't find something. What's inside this?

NIALL. Don't you open it.

MILDRED. I haven't seen it before. (she tries to open it)

NIALL. I said DON'T. If you so much as open the lid a fraction...

MILDRED. (laughing) You'll what? (she again tries to open the box)

NIALL. I'll smash your museum to smithereens and fling the bits down into the street!

MILDRED. You wouldn't dare!

NIALL. Wouldn't I? Watch me. (he strides over to the glass-topped cabinet and snatches off the shawl)

MILDRED. (running towards him) NO!

NIALL. You leave my box alone then.

MILDRED. Put my shawl back.

(They glare at each other. Eventually NIALL,

20

letting out his breath in a long sigh, covers the
glass case with the shawl)

NIALL. You're not to touch my box.

MILDRED. (quietly) That's your carpentry box isn't
it?

(NIALL picks up his tie and stands in front of the
mirror)

I said, isn't it?

NIALL. No.

MILDRED. Yes it is.

NIALL. I'm not going to argue.

(Silence)

MILDRED. (sitting on the bed) What IS in there?

NIALL. Something which belongs to me.

MILDRED. You're not going to tell me?

NIALL. (struggling with his tie) No.

MILDRED. You will eventually.

NIALL. I will not.

MILDRED. I shall worm it out of you.

NIALL. Not this time.

MILDRED. I shall keep on until you tell me.

NIALL. (struggling with his tie) I'm not listening.

MILDRED. I won't offer to do your tie.

NIALL. I can manage thank you.

MILDRED. I'll never tie it for you again. Ever.

NIALL. I'm weeping for you.

(Silence)

MILDRED. I shall go out and buy a hammer AND some
nails.

NIALL. (turning, his tie untied) YOU? Go out shopping?
You haven't been outside this flat in months. MONTHS!

MILDRED. I have too.

NIALL. You have not. You're even too scared to put
the waste bin out on the front steps. Go out? That's
a laugh.

(He turns back to the mirror. Silence)

Anyway, it's Sunday. The shops will be shut.

MILDRED. How d'you know it's Sunday?

NIALL. Because... (becoming agitated and flapping his
arms) Because it FEELS like Sunday.

MILDRED. But you don't know for certain.

NIALL. OF COURSE I KNOW! Anyway, what the hell
does it matter what day of the week it is? You
NEVER go out.

MILDRED. I shall today.

NIALL. I've heard that before.

MILDRED. I'm going to buy a hammer and some nails
  for those curtains.

NIALL. You do that.

MILDRED. I will.

NIALL. (taunting her) You'd better hurry before you
  change your mind or before you get one of those
  turns of yours.

MILDRED. I'll go now. (she stands and walks towards
  the door) I'm going.

NIALL. The sooner the better.

  (MILDRED, leaving the door ajar, walks quietly
  from the room. NIALL, concentrating on his tie,
  does not realise that MILDRED has left the room,
  throwing off her nightie. He turns. Seeing the
  landing door opens, he frowns)

  Mildred?

  (Not receiving an answer, he turns. Seeing
  MILDRED's nightdress on the floor and the door
  still open, he immediately jumps to the right
  conclusion)

  YE GODS!

  (Picking up MILDRED's nightdress, he runs out of the
  room and down the passage, shouting)

  COME BACK! IDIOT! COME HERE!

MILDRED. I'm going to the shops.

NIALL. Not like that, you're not. Put this back on.
  Quickly! PUT - IT - ON!

MILDRED. Leave me alone! LET GO OF ME!

NIALL. Get back into that room!

MILDRED. No! OW! YOU PIG! (a door slams) I
hate you!

NIALL. Get-back-into-that-room!

MILDRED. Pig!

(Silence)

NIALL. Go on! Back!

(MILDRED, in her nightdress and rubbing her arm,
followed closely by NIALL, re-enters the room.
MILDRED sits down heavily on the bed)

MILDRED. You bruised me.

NIALL. WHAT - THE - HELL - GOT - INTO - YOU?

MILDRED. I'm bruised.

NIALL. It's lucky for you old man Haines wasn't on the
prowl - he'd have had you up against the bannisters
in a flash.

MILDRED. I'm black and blue.

NIALL. You can be arrested for walking the streets
naked - or didn't you know?

MILDRED. I don't care.

NIALL. (shaking his head) I don't understand you. I
really don't. Some days you tart yourself up - spend
hours making yourself look decent - you get all
ready to go out - hat, gloves, overcoat, scarf,
shopping bag - the lot - and then - suddenly - for no
reason at all you decide NOT to go out and climb
straight back into bed. But today? Today you get

an urgent desire to parade down the High Street STARK NAKED! Where's the logic in that? For months you won't go out dressed and now suddenly you want to go out naked!

(MILDRED, her head bent, is examining her bruised arm)

And it isn't even raining!

MILDRED. WHAT DO YOU MEAN?

NIALL. You tell me.

MILDRED. I can't do anything without you spying on me all the time.

NIALL. You came back soaked to the skin.

MILDRED. You always have to be looking at me.

NIALL. Dripping all over the floor...

MILDRED. As if I'd done something wrong.

NIALL. With an ecstatic look on your face.

MILDRED. You won't let me be happy.

NIALL. I know why.

MILDRED. If I'm like I am, it's because of you.

NIALL. Because of HIM!

MILDRED. You won't let me be myself.

NIALL. Alone, you said. At the cinema, you said.

MILDRED. A woman's every right to her independence. Even if she is married.

NIALL. And you stood in a puddle. Just there. (pointing)

Soaked to the skin. Lost your knickers, you said.
They were in your handbag!

MILDRED. What if they were!

NIALL. The rain reminds you of him!

MILDRED. That was thirteen years ago!

> (And, putting her hands to her head, MILDRED
> twists and throws herself face down on to the bed,
> sobbing loudly. NIALL, making a despairing
> gesture, begins to move restlessly about the room)

NIALL. I'm sorry, Mildred.

MILDRED. (her face buried in the bedclothes and still
sobbing) You would have to bring HIM into it,
wouldn't you. ANYTHING to hurt me. (she raises her
head) It was thirteen years ago. THIRTEEN YEARS!
(and she collapses again)

NIALL. I'm sorry, Mildred. Why don't you get back into
bed? Mmm? Come on. (he helps MILDRED to get
under the bedclothes) There's a good girl. (he
leans over MILDRED to kiss her, but she buries her
face in the pillow)

MILDRED. Get away from me!

NIALL. Would you like breakfast in bed? Eh? (he
begins to tuck in the blankets) You like that.

MILDRED. (still quietly sobbing) I only wanted to buy
some, some nails - for the curtains. And a hammer.

NIALL. Don't worry. I'll do the curtains.

MILDRED. Do it now.

NIALL. You want me to nail them down now?

MILDRED. (excitedly) Yes. Would you? Please.

26

Please, Niall. Do it now. I want you to do it more than anything. (and then, cajolingly) Do it just to please me, Niall. P-l-e-a-s-e darling.

NIALL. If you wish.

MILDRED. And can I watch you do it?

NIALL. A man at work? Why not.

(NIALL picks up the wooden chair and carries it to the wardrobe)

Why don't more women stand around watching holes being dug?

(He stands on the chair and gropes about on the top of the wardrobe)

You'd think they'd be attracted by the half-naked men showing off their sunburnt backs as they pick into the virgin tarmac.

(He holds up hammer and tacks, and grins)

But they're taught not to, as little girls.

(He gets down off the chair and, crossing to the window, begins to arrange the folds in the drawn curtains)

Instead, they become pole squatters and we have to look up to them.

MILDRED. Make sure the edges are properly together.

NIALL. Is that decent?

MILDRED. (appreciatively) Yes, that looks nice.

(NIALL bangs in a tack to hold them together)

NIALL. I'd like to have seen Suckling's face when you

walked into his shop stark naked to buy some tacks.
(he begins to tack down one side of the curtain) His
glasses would have steamed over.

MILDRED. Perhaps I never intended to go.

NIALL. He'd have taken an age to count out the tacks – one
at a time – slowly, so's he got a proper look at you.

MILDRED. I wasn't aware I hadn't got a stitch on...

NIALL. Then, as likely as not, he'd have dropped the bag
of tacks – accidentally on purpose, of course, just as
he was handing them to you, so's to watch you bend
over and pick it up.

(Having tacked the side, NIALL stands back)

MILDRED. Don't forget the bottom.

NIALL. The memory of that would have boggled his mind
for the rest of his life. (and he begins to tack along
the bottom of the curtains)

MILDRED. And tack it along the top.

NIALL. But the rings hold it firm.

MILDRED. You promised.

NIALL. (shrugging) Very well.

(He fetches the wooden chair and stands on it)

I saw a man once.

(He bangs home a tack)

A long time ago.

(And another)

He was running down Queensway in his birthday suit.

28

His arms were going like pistons and his knees were up to his chin.

(He bangs in another tack)

Belting down the road he was. All he'd got on was a pair of tatty white pumps. And do you know what? All the women laughed.

(He gets down, shifts the chair along and mounts it again)

They dropped their shopping and doubled up with laughter.

(He bangs in a tack)

Even the sour-faced ones. But not the men. They didn't laugh. Poker-faced - the lot of them. Some even blushed. Strange, that.

(He hammers in another tack)

It was the men who were disturbed.

(He bangs home the final tack)

Now if it had been the other way about - if it had been you, or some other women, running down the street stark naked and slopping about all over the place, it would have been the men who would have become hysterical with laughter and slapped each other on the back because of what they'd seen. (he gets down off the chair) It's all a question of sexual clanship.

MILDRED. And the other. (she points to the edge of the curtain)

NIALL. (beginning to tack down the right hand side of the curtain) I've always wondered what made that man run down Queensway in his birthday suit.

(He bangs in a tack)

I don't suppose it was to fetch a bag of tacks.

(He hammers home another tack)

I expect it was the reverse of what he really wanted
to do.

(And another tack)

Like you.

(He hammers in the final tack, stands back and turns
to MILDRED)

Is that what you wanted?

MILDRED. It's lovely. All enclosed.

NIALL. Good. (putting the hammer and tacks on the
    floor and walking towards the bed) What about a
    kiss, then? (MILDRED puts out her arms towards
    him and they kiss. Briefly)

MILDRED. Thank you Niall darling. You've made me very
    happy. (NIALL leans towards her for another kiss)
    No, no. You've had your kiss.

NIALL. (walking round the bed) I suppose you'll want me
    to sew together where the curtains join.

MILDRED. I'll do that.

NIALL. (surprised) Oh. Well. Don't forget to leave
    a little hole to urinate through.

MILDRED. I'm not so stupid. WHAT DID YOU SAY?

(Silence)

I ASKED YOU WHAT YOU SAID TO ME JUST THEN!

NIALL. We'll suffocate, you know.

MILDRED. You said something which I didn't quite
catch.

NIALL. They'll find us dead from suffocation. No air'll
be able to get in. Or out. Suicide pact, they'll say.
A middle aged man and his child wife...

MILDRED. I'm not a child!

NIALL. It would sound better in the papers. Or. Old man
and young, attractive woman kill themselves. Lovers
found dead in bed.

MILDRED. (with contempt) Lovers! HA. That'll be
the day.

NIALL. How else could they describe us? Bosom pals
die in same bed. Was it suicide pact? Due to
over-crowding, says coroner. Lack of breathing
room in Borough, says angry councillor. Was
Bayswater brunette imprisoned in Paddington hovel?
Riddle of missing wedding ring still unsolved.

MILDRED. It dropped down the loo. I told you.

NIALL. Our crime reporter investigates and reveals all.
You'll see. It'll be in all the Sundays.

MILDRED. If you're so worried about suffocating, why
don't you open the window a fraction?

NIALL. And HOW am I meant to do that?

MILDRED. (flinging back the bedclothes and getting out
of bed) You're helpless, aren't you? (going towards
the window) Like a great big baby. (she puts her
arm between the curtains and, after much grunting
and muttering, succeeds in opening a window)
THERE. Was that SO difficult?

(She climbs back into bed)

WAS it? Baby.

NIALL. For you? No. Simplicity itself. A faultless,
painless delivery. I congratulate you. Hail Mary.

(Pulling his tie out of his pocket, he walks to the
mirror)

It would be far more practical to paste brown paper
over the glass. No one could see in and we could
always open the windows when we wanted.

MILDRED. BROWN PAPER OVER THE GLASS? ARE
YOU MAD? WHAT WOULD THE NEIGHBOURS
THINK?

NIALL. Seeing the curtains drawn all day - every day,
they must think something. Probably that we're
having it off all the time.

MILDRED. PIG!

NIALL. That you've got a headache? More likely that
we've got something to hide. Like a slave. Perhaps
they think we sit about all day. Drugged.

MILDRED. Don't be so stupid.

NIALL. Watching blue films, then?

MILDRED. Pig.

NIALL. All right. One of us works nights. Who cares?
Maybe they think we're dead. God knows, there are
times when I think I am.

MILDRED. I'm not having them gawp.

NIALL. Gawp at what? Not counting the basement, we're
three floors up. How can anyone see in?

MILDRED. What about the people opposite? Across the
street. They go up on the roof in summer. I've seen

one of them with binoculars. That fat man who's always in his vest.

NIALL. (looking round the room) What is there to see? There's nothing in here that could possibly interest him.

MILDRED. Now you're trying to insult me. I know you don't think I'm very attractive... but I'm not going to expose myself.

NIALL. No one's asking you to. Anyway, how often does anyone go up on the roof to sun themselves? Twice a year?

MILDRED. They don't have to go up on the roof to see in.

NIALL. Buy some net curtains then. Most of the windows opposite have them. You can't see into their rooms from here. Can you? Have you ever seen into their rooms? Well? Have you?

MILDRED. What are you suggesting? That I spend my time like some filthy voyeur...

NIALL. I'm not SUGGESTING anything. I'm TELLING you. BUY SOME NET CURTAINING!

MILDRED. And what about the sun? You can see through net when the sun shines on it. And WE get most of the sun.

NIALL. It doesn't bloody shine in this room.

MILDRED. It would excite you to think they could see me through the net.

NIALL. There's mould growing on the walls.

MILDRED. Like that disgusting transparent nightdress you tried to get me to wear.

NIALL. And our skin's turning the colour of cheese. All the veins standing out blue.

MILDRED. I wouldn't be seen dead in such a thing.

NIALL. We've become corpses.

MILDRED. I'm not parading myself for inspection.

NIALL. What did you say?

MILDRED. I've still got my pride.

NIALL. Good. Then polish up the windows and buy some net curtains. From the outside it looks as if this room is inhabited by some old spinster.

MILDRED. I'm not having a window cleaner!

NIALL. (turning away in exasperation) Damn you George Formby - you - buck-toothed banjo-playing Lancastrian bogey-man!

MILDRED. It's not for nothing men tell those dirty stories about what the window cleaner saw! I'm not having some lecherous idiot huffing on my window panes and grinning in at me.

NIALL. Don't then. Don't. DON't!

MILDRED. I've a sense of decency.

NIALL. I'm not interested.

MILDRED. That's typical. You don't care about my feelings. How I might feel. It doesn't matter to you. You'd stand at the window stark naked. You'd enjoy that.

NIALL. When have I ever exposed myself at the window?

MILDRED. I expect you've thought about it.

NIALL. Oh yes. Often. Daily.

MILDRED. YOU SEE! I WAS RIGHT! It's just the sort of filthy thing you'd like to do. MEN! Just because you've got a miserable little thing sticking out in front of you, you think all the world wants to see it. But take it away, and what have you got?

NIALL. An ugly wound.

MILDRED. You're like a lot of small smelly boys the way you all seize on every opportunity to show it off.

NIALL. An unhealed wound.

MILDRED. Priding yourself and thinking it's beautiful.

NIALL. YOUR wound.

MILDRED. It's UGLY.

NIALL. The eternal wound of which you are so ashamed.

MILDRED. Imagining everyone wants to see a thing like that.

NIALL. So you draw the edges together and suture them with nails.

MILDRED. It ought to be chopped off when it's finished its usefulness.

NIALL. And while you sit about feeling inadequate, two people smoulder to death; hating each others' guts.

MILDRED. What are you babbling about?

NIALL. A subject I wouldn't dream of mentioning in front of you, my dear.

MILDRED. I know all about man's talk.

NIALL. Yes, dear.

MILDRED. I've seen them with their hands in their pockets laughing. Red faced and bulging eyed at some filthy joke.

NIALL. They never fail to be amused.

MILDRED. Even a wife's not sacred over a pint of beer when it comes to out-boasting the other wet-lipped pigs of men.

NIALL. We all sup from a common trough.

MILDRED. I expect they went into hysterics when you told them about my birth mark.

NIALL. You cannot joke about stigmatas.

MILDRED. Everything is a joke to you men.

NIALL. I'll make some coffee.

MILDRED. And the more intimate and grotesque the details, the more excited you become.

NIALL. And we'll have toast and marmalade.

MILDRED. We've not enough holes for all your phantasies.

NIALL. Or bubble and squeak?

MILDRED. We're unloved carcasses to be slapped and pulled into meatless shapes.

NIALL. Bacon?

MILDRED. To be slobbered over, gulped and devoured, regurgitated and to be masticated all over again and again.

NIALL. DO YOU WANT BREAKFAST?

MILDRED. You're not listening. You NEVER listen.

(NIALL goes into the kitchen. Sound of crashing)

When I'VE got something to say, you don't pay attention.

NIALL. (from the kitchen) HAVE YOU SEEN THE MATCHES?

(Silence)

I SAID HAVE YOU... WHAT THE?

(NIALL storms into the room)

YOU'VE GONE AND NAILED UP THE CURTAINS IN THE KITCHEN!

MILDRED. Yes.

NIALL. Good God, woman, where's the sense in that? There's only a brick wall facing that window. The back of the house opposite is brick from top to bottom. Not a window in it.

MILDRED. Then you haven't looked.

NIALL. I've seen the bricks.

MILDRED. And you find that interesting to look at?

NIALL. Yes.

MILDRED. Nasty brown bricks?

NIALL. It's better than total darkness and having to feel your way around in there.

MILDRED. You'd find it interesting looking up someone's nose.

NIALL. I can't find any matches.

MILDRED. There's a box in the small cupboard.

(NIALL turns and walks towards the kitchen but stops suddenly and turns to face MILDRED)

NIALL. Wait - a - minute... If you didn't know where I kept the tacks and hammer... WHO NAILED THEM UP FOR YOU?

MILDRED. I nailed them down myself.

NIALL. Did you get Langley to do it for you?

MILDRED. It was much easier than I thought.

NIALL. Has he been coming without my knowing?

MILDRED. It didn't take long. Well. Longer than you'd have taken.

NIALL. Have you two been up to something behind my back?

MILDRED. I just banged and banged and banged....

NIALL. Back at your old tricks again, I suppose.

MILDRED. ... USING THE HAMMER. Like you do.

NIALL. Making me suffer. Humiliating me.

MILDRED. It was great fun doing it.

NIALL. Pretending you've no liking for it, except with him.

MILDRED. I was so exhausted afterwards, I made myself a cup of tea.

NIALL. If ever I come across that Langley, I'll wring his bloody neck. D'YOU HEAR?

MILDRED. Langley won't come again.

NIALL. Not with you he won't.

MILDRED. Langley's dead.

NIALL. My heart bleeds. When did he die?

MILDRED. Langley's passed out of my life.

NIALL. EVERYBODY passes out of your life sooner or later, but when did Langley go?

MILDRED. I did as you told me. I forbade him write or to ever try and see me again.

NIALL. So he's not dead?

MILDRED. You killed off anything there might have been between us. Just as you kill off all my friends.

NIALL. WHAT FRIENDS?

MILDRED. You turn everybody against me.

NIALL. I paint you in glowing colours...

MILDRED. I know what you say to them behind my back.

NIALL. ... because I'm ashamed to let them know how things are between us.

MILDRED. Even the milkman looks at me in an odd way.

NIALL. But they use their eyes.

MILDRED. And the postman. As if they suspect something.

NIALL. They put two and two together.

MILDRED. I'm sure they gossip with that Mrs. Frigg...

NIALL. But think it's me that's odd for sticking to you.

MILDRED. ... who's just like that. (she crosses two fingers) With old man Haines.

NIALL. Old Man Haines? He's not a friend.

MILDRED. He's a dirty pig. Touched me on the bottom once.

NIALL. You never told me.

MILDRED. I've heard the both of you sniggering out on the landing.

NIALL. Passing the time of day... but you never told me.

MILDRED. Swopping tales like men do.

NIALL. Why didn't you tell me?

MILDRED. Tell you? Tell you what? That you'd put him up to it?

NIALL. TO TOUCHING YOU UP? YOU'RE MAD! OLD MAN HAINES HAS GOT A STRING OF CONVICTIONS AS LONG AS YOUR ARM FOR...

MILDRED. (suddenly kneeling up in bed, alarmed) WHAT'S THAT SMELL?

NIALL. Don't try and change the subject.

MILDRED. THAT SMELL! It's gas. GAS! YOU'VE LEFT THE GAS ON!

NIALL. (sniffing) Gas? GAS! Oh my God. THE GAS. I FORGOT TO TURN THE GAS OFF!

(He turns and runs into the kitchen. There is the sound of tearing cloth and a window being smashed. MILDRED stands wide-eyed on the bed, a corner of one sheet held up to her mouth. NIALL rushes in from the kitchen and up to the window. He tears at the curtains, trying to get to the window)

DAMN YOU AND YOUR BLASTED CURTAINS!

MILDRED. DON'T TEAR THEM! (and she jumps off the
    bed to stop him)

NIALL. (pushing her away) YOU DON'T WANT TO BE
    GASSED, DO YOU?

MILDRED. BUT THE CURTAINS, NIALL!

    (NIALL gives MILDRED another push which sends her
    sprawling on the bed. Tearing the curtains, he
    opens the window. MILDRED lies sobbing on the bed
    while NIALL walks about the room flapping his arms.
    He picks up an article of MILDRED's underclothing
    and waves it about in huge circles)

NIALL. That's clearing it.

    (Seeing MILDRED sobbing, NIALL utters an oath and
    flings the undergarment at her. It lands on her
    head. MILDRED looks up, sees what it is, and
    throws it from her)

MILDRED. YOU FILTHY PIG!

NIALL. (after glaring at MILDRED) I'm off. (he
    searches for his jacket, finds it and struggles into
    it)

MILDRED. WHAT ABOUT THE CURTAINS?

NIALL. That's your problem.

    (MILDRED, with a shriek, buries herself under the
    bedclothes)

    I'm going down to the shops. Do you want anything?

    (Silence)

    Have you made out a shopping list for me?

MILDRED. It's in the kitchen under the tea caddy.

(NIALL goes into the kitchen and returns a moment
later with a piece of paper)

NIALL. This it?

(Silence)

I'm off then.

(NIALL glances round the room, feels in his pockets
and exits, banging the door. MILDRED sits up,
looks at the window and then at the door. Sniffing,
wiping her eyes on the sheet, she gets out of bed
slowly. Seeing the red wooden box on the floor, she
tenses. Her mood changing swiftly, she tiptoes to
the door and, putting her ear to it, listens.
Then, opening the door cautiously, she peers out on
to the landing. Closing the door she runs quickly to
the window. Making certain that she cannot be seen,
she looks down into the street. A smile appears on
her face when she sees NIALL walking briskly away
from the house. Turning, MILDRED runs to the
box and kneels down beside it. The box is locked.
MILDRED scrambles to her feet, picks up the
hammer from near to the window and, returning to
the box, stands over it, gleeful anticipation on her
face. MILDRED struggles for a long time, trying to
prize open the lid of the red box. When it becomes
obvious that despite her efforts the lid cannot be
prized open, she loses her temper and hammers the
box with all her strength. The lid springs open and,
with a cry of triumph, MILDRED looks inside. The
box is empty. In a blind rage she proceeds to destroy
the red box)

Scene Two

(Two o'clock in the afternoon of the same day.
MILDRED is in bed reading a paperback novel. The
pieces of the broken red box are nowhere to be seen.

The curtains have been removed from the window and
brown paper pasted over the glass, making the room
even gloomier and depressing in the light of the one,
unshaded electric bulb. The door leading out onto the
landing opens and NIALL puts his head round it.
Then he taps the door)

NIALL. Are we respectable?

(He turns to someone behind him. NIALL enters,
closely followed by GLADYS SPENDLOVE who is
carrying a suitcase)

I couldn't get much. It IS Sunday. Only the dairy
was open.

(NIALL holds up a bottle of milk and a brown paper
bag. GLADYS closes the door)

It's very dark, isn't it? Oh!

(Seeing the brown paper pasted over the window,
he walks over to look. GLADYS stands nervously
by the door)

You've been busy, haven't you?

MILDRED. I got tired of waiting. What would have
    happened if someone had taken it into their head to
    call on us?

NIALL. No one would be so daft. Tea?

(MILDRED, for the first time, notices GLADYS. She
does not conceal her surprise)

MILDRED. NIALL!

(But NIALL has disappeared into the kitchen.
MILDRED scowls at GLADYS. GLADYS shifts her
weight to her other foot and clears her throat
nervously. NIALL returns)

Who's she?

NIALL. Oh. Yes. That's Gladys. (to GLADYS) Take
off your coat, Glad. Tea won't be long. Make
yourself at home.

(Still standing close to the door, GLADYS puts down
her suitcase and takes off her coat. Draping it over
her arm, she smiles weakly at MILDRED. MILDRED
worms her way down into the bed. NIALL returns
to the kitchen with some of the crockery which had
slid off the trunk. He returns almost immediately,
withdrawing a newspaper from her pocket. He
throws it to MILDRED)

Here, CATCH.

(MILDRED catches the newspaper, opens it at the
centre page and holds it up in front of her so that she
is lost from sight. GLADYS allows her eyes to wander
round the room. Suddenly, MILDRED crumples one
side of the newspaper and stares at her. NIALL
returns with two cups and saucers. He puts them on
the trunk.

NIALL. I met Glad on the station platform.

MILDRED. GLAD?

NIALL. Yes, Glad. Oh. Mildred. This is Gladys
Spendlove. Gladys, this is my... This is Mildred.

GLADYS. How d'you do Mrs. Scringeour.

MILDRED. Wringe.

GLADYS. I beg your pardon?

MILDRED. Wringe is my own name. I prefer it to
Scringeour.

GLADYS. (advancing. Perhaps two steps) Your
husband...

44

MILDRED. MISTER SCRINGEOUR.

(Silence)

NIALL. Yes. Well.

(To GLADYS, as he rights the fallen chair:)

Would you like to come and sit down?

GLADYS. Thank you.

(She sits. NIALL goes into the kitchen. MILDRED and GLADYS continue to glare at each other. NIALL enters carrying a teapot and a bowl of sugar)

NIALL. (to GLADYS) Do you take sugar in your tea?

GLADYS. (giggling) I'm trying to slim.

NIALL. No sugar then.

MILDRED. Mister Scringeour likes his women fat. They have to have bosoms like balloons and backsides like sacks of corn to please Mister Scringeour. Don't they, Niall? You like your women fat.

NIALL. You're not fat, my dear.

MILDRED. That's why he despises me Miss Spendlove, because I'm normal. Because I'm not abundantly milked like some grotesque mother Earth and keep my tail tucked in.

NIALL. (to GLADYS) Milk, Miss Spendlove?

GLADYS. Please. A little.

MILDRED. What are WE going to drink from. There are only two cups.

NIALL. I thought you and I could drink from the same cup.

MILDRED. Don't be disgusting!

NIALL. I'll have it AFTER you've drunk from it.

MILDRED. I want my own cup.

NIALL. Oh, very well. I'll have my tea in a jam jar.

GLADYS. You have this cup, Mister Scringeour. I'll
rinse it out when you've finished. I don't mind
waiting. (she begins to pour the tea)

MILDRED. She's quite plump, Niall.

GLADYS. (rising with a cup) Mrs. Wringe...

MILDRED. MISS.

GLADYS. I beg your pardon. Miss Wringe. Your tea.
(she hands the tea to MILDRED who accepts it
without grace)

(NIALL takes his tea) Now. Shall I divide the
cake?

NIALL. Please. You be mother.

(GLADYS smiles. MILDRED snorts down her nose)

GLADYS. (as she cuts the cake) Should we have
plates.

NIALL. We won't bother with plates. Fingers will do.

MILDRED. He's no manners Miss Spendlove. He uses
his fingers for everything. He's all fingers. I saw
him pick his nose a moment ago. (pause) I'll have
a plate. AND a fork.

(GLADYS gets up and goes into the kitchen. She
returns with a plate and a fork. Skilfully, she
manoeuvres a slice of cake onto the plate and
carries it over to MILDRED)

GLADYS. Miss Wringe. (MILDRED takes the proffered cake)

MILDRED. How nice to be waited upon. Such a change.

GLADYS. (smiling) Thank you. (she cuts herself a slice of cake and, holding it in her fingers, eats it)

MILDRED. What were you doing at the station?

NIALL. (as GLADYS turns and tries to swallow quickly, imagining it is to her MILDRED's question is addressed) I was looking up the times of the trains to Liverpool. (cramming cake down)

MILDRED. Off on one of your long trips again? While I stay here cooped up on my own. Little you care.

NIALL. I shall only be gone for a week. Less perhaps.

MILDRED. (sarcastically) BUSINESS, I suppose.

NIALL. I have to earn some money, Mildred. We can't always be living on tea and cake. And there's the rent. The electric light bills. That (he indicates the glowing bulb) burns up a small fortune. It costs money to live. I must go to Liverpool and earn some.

MILDRED. And leave me on my own.

NIALL. The one time when you did come with me - or rather, the time when you got as far as the station, was a disaster.

MILDRED. You might have asked me if I wanted to go.

NIALL. To give you the pleasure of refusing?

MILDRED. I don't CHOOSE to stay alone!

NIALL. Well, you won't be this time.

47

MILDRED. What d'you mean?

NIALL. That's why I brought Gladys along.

MILDRED. What has Gladys got to do with it?

NIALL. I thought she could stay here while I was away.
It would be company for you.

MILDRED. WHAT!

(She slides quickly out of bed)

You THOUGHT? Thought I'd.... You've got a
damned nerve bringing somebody I don't even know
... someone I've never met before... some old...
old TROLLOP you picked up at the Railway station
and bringing her back to the flat! To STAY, you
said? Oh, no. No. You get her out of here,
quick!

(GLADYS looks decidedly ill at ease. She makes as
if to get up but NIALL indicates she should stay
where she is. GLADYS sits nervously on the edge
of the seat on the lop-sided chair)

NIALL. She's destitute.

MILDRED. She looks it!

(For the first time, GLADYS looks at MILDRED
defiantly and gives a tug to her smart suit)

NIALL. So? None of us can help our circumstances.

MILDRED. You can get up to all the dirty tricks you
like in Liverpool - but not in my flat. You've got a
damned cheek bringing a prostitute back with you,
I must say.

GLADYS. (standing) I AM NOT A PROSTITUTE!

MILDRED. No? Well, he seems to think you are. And

48

he's got a nose for that sort of thing.

NIALL. I said DESTITUTE, not prostitute. Idiot.

(There is a moment's silence before MILDRED
falls back on the bed laughing. NIALL glances at
GLADYS and shrugs his shoulders as much as to say
'I told you so'. He motions GLADYS to be seated.
She turns down the corners of her mouth. NIALL
makes calming motions with his hands and GLADYS
sits. MILDRED, recovered, props herself up on
one elbow)

MILDRED. That was a laugh, wasn't it?

NIALL. Gladys has been turned out of her room. She's
no money and no job.

MILDRED. What were you doing on the railway station?

GLADYS. The waiting-room was warm.

MILDRED. Oh.

NIALL. Can she stay?

MILDRED. Don't be silly. Where's she going to
sleep?

NIALL. There are two mattresses on that bed. Gladys
can have one of them on the floor.

MILDRED. And the blankets?

NIALL. There's too many on the bed already.

MILDRED. (shaking her head) She's not staying here!

NIALL. She's staying.

MILDRED. NO - SHE - ISN'T.

NIALL. Tonight she is. I promised.

MILDRED. I'm not sharing my room with a stranger!
And that's final!

GLADYS. (standing and putting her coat back on) I
think if you don't mind, Mister Scringeour, I'd better
be running along...

NIALL. SIT DOWN. You're staying.

GLADYS. No. Really. Thank you all the same. It was
nice of you to think you could help, but... Well.
Never mind. A pity though. I would have liked to
have stayed. Your flat's so cosy, Miss, er, Miss
Wringe. Intimate. And so feminine. It appeals to
me very much. Just the sort of room I could have
been happy in if... but there. Never mind. I'm sure
we could have got on well together. (to NIALL) I'd
like to powder my nose before I go. May I? In there,
is it? (she points to the bathroom door)

NIALL. (nodding) Of course.

GLADYS. Thank you. (she goes into the bathroom and
closes the door)

NIALL. (putting some crumbs in his mouth) I think you
could have been a little more hospitable to Miss
Spendlove. She's down on her luck.

MILDRED. I'd like to have seen how you would have
reacted if I'd turned up with a strange man I'd picked
up and calmly announced that he was going to stay
with us.

NIALL. I was only thinking of you! Dammit Mildred, I
... Oh what's the use.

(Silence)

It seems I can never do the right thing.

MILDRED. That is an understatement.

(GLADYS comes out of the bathroom pulling on a pair of gloves. She closes the bathroom door behind her)

GLADYS. (to MILDRED) I don't like all those mirrors in your bathroom. They are so... so. Well. It's hardly nice, is it?

(MILDRED stares at GLADYS, then looks at NIALL and smirks)

MILDRED. You don't approve of them, Miss Spendlove?

GLADYS. It's positively indecent. I certainly don't want to stay if that's the sort of bathroom you have.

MILDRED. (beaming at NIALL) THAT'S EXACTLY WHAT I THINK MISS SPENDLOVE! (to GLADYS:) Personally, I always drape towels over them whenever I go in there. Don't I, Niall?

GLADYS. How, how very cultured of you.

NIALL. CULTURED?

GLADYS. I thought I wasn't mistaken. You're sensitive. Like me. The kind of upbringing one's had always shows through in the end, don't you think?

MILDRED. Very true. As you might have guessed, it was Mister Scringeour who insisted upon putting mirrors in the bathroom.

NIALL. (pointing to the small mirror) How can I see myself in that damned thing?

MILDRED. He'd have them in here if he could. Over the bed of course.

GLADYS. (shuddering) Men are disgusting.

MILDRED. It's so nice to meet someone who has the same views as oneself. It's very reassuring.

NIALL. I knew a woman once...

GLADYS. We all have the same problem, Miss
   Wringe. We women, that is.

NIALL. This woman I knew...

MILDRED. Please Gladys. Call me Mildred.

NIALL. She was nearly fifty...

GLADYS. (removing her gloves) In a man's world, it's
   extremely difficult for us - the few who haven't
   already been corrupted by men, it is extremely
   difficult...

NIALL. WILL YOU LISTEN! (MILDRED and GLADYS
   turn towards NIALL with disapproving frowns) Thank
   you. She was nearly fifty.

MILDRED. Who was?

NIALL. This woman I know.

MILDRED. I don't think you told me about her. What
   was her name?

NIALL. (groaning) Mrs. Stammers. You know her.
   She's nearly fifty. Lives in Northumberland Avenue.
   In the pink house. Well, she told me she'd never
   seen herself naked in a full length mirror.

GLADYS. I shouldn't think she'd want to if she was
   nearly fifty.

MILDRED. How right you are.

NIALL. But you don't understand. She'd never looked
   at herself. Ever. Not once in her whole life could
   she remember seeing herself naked.

MILDRED. So?

GLADYS. What is there to look at?

MILDRED. Exactly.

NIALL. But she didn't even want to!

GLADYS. No more would I.

NIALL. But you can't go through life... you're not just head, hands and feet. THERE'S ALL THE REST OF YOU! Aren't you ever curious to know what the rest of you's like?

GLADYS. Certainly not.

NIALL. Not even to see if you're putting on too much weight? Ageing? Sagging in the wrong places?

MILDRED. Don't be filthy, Niall. Really.

NIALLY. I'M NOT BEING FILTHY! GOD! Aren't you proud of your body? Or curious? That when you stand in front of a mirror naked, you are seeing the real you. As you really are. Aren't you even interested?

GLADYS. I'd much rather not see, thank you.

MILDRED. Neither would I. You're very vulgar, Niall. Crude. And to think you talk like that in front of strangers. A lady too. And our guest. (drawing GLADYS to one side) I must apologise for Mister Scringeour's lack of manners. You haven't had a cup of tea yet. Use my cup. And let me take your coat.

NIALL. (as MILDRED helps GLADYS off with her coat) You won't try and understand, will you? Either of you. You're frightened of what you will see. Ashamed of your own sex.

MILDRED. It's all so unimportant. (laying GLADYS's coat over the back of a chair) And if you're going to Liverpool Niall, don't you think you ought to hurry up and pack your case?

(NIALL snorts and gets up to find his suitcase.
Laying it open on the bed, he flings his clothes in
without bothering to fold them; glancing from time
to time at the two women who are deep in conversation
in the kitchen doorway. As he stands looking down
into the suitcase trying to puzzle out what else he
might need while he is away, the two women walk
back to the centre of the room. MILDRED motions
GLADYS, who is holding a cup of tea, towards the
armchair and sits down on the wooden chair
opposite her. NIALL closes his suitcase and walks
over to MILDRED with his tie)

NIALL. Would you knot this for me please Mildred?

(MILDRED looks up at him, smiles and turns to
GLADYS)

MILDRED. Whenever he goes away, I have to knot his
ties for him. Silly, isn't it? A grown man, and
still has trouble with his tie.

NIALL. One day I'll do it for myself. Then you'll be
sorry.

MILDRED. (to NIALL) Kneel down then.

NIALL. (glancing at GLADYS but addressing MILDRED)
Can't you do it standing up?

MILDRED. They imagine we NEED them, when really it's
the other way about. I'd be quite happy if there weren't
any men.

NIALL. My tie.

MILDRED. Don't be so impatient. Kneel down.

NIALL. But...

MILDRED. KNEEL!

NIALL. Oh - very well.

(He kneels in front of her. MILDRED, over his head makes eyes at GLADYS who barely restrains herself from giggling. While MILDRED ties NIALL's tie, he gazes up at the ceiling)

MILDRED. We only need men for breeding purposes, and God knows, I've never had any desire for a child, so what's the use of a man to me? To any of us? THERE. (she turns down NIALL's collar) What do you say?

NIALL. (rising to his feet) Thank you.

MILDRED. Thank you what?

NIALL. Thank you Mildred for tying my tie.

MILDRED. And what time is your train?

NIALL. Five ten.

MILDRED. And what's the time now?

GLADYS. (looking at her wrist watch) A quarter past four.

MILDRED. You'd better hurry then.

NIALL. It only takes six minutes to walk to the station.

MILDRED. But you don't want to miss your train, do you?

NIALL. I can take a hint. Are you coming Miss Spend-love?

MILDRED. Gladys is staying.

NIALL. (surprised) Are you?

MILDRED. Of course she is. I invited her. (GLADYS

smiles)

NIALL. Well, in that case... (he looks about him, at a loss to know what to do or say. He picks up his suitcase, feels his tie, pats his pocket and sniffs) Well, I'm off then I suppose.

MILDRED. Good.

NIALL. See you in five days time. (MILDRED deliberately turns her back on him as she rises to her feet) You're sure you'll be alright?

MILDRED. For goodness sake, go.

NIALL. Yes. Well. Goodbye, Miss Spendlove.

GLADYS. Shall I make another pot of tea, Mildred?

MILDRED. That would be lovely.

MILDRED. (to GLADYS who is walking towards the kitchen) We'll have toast. (to NIALL) Oh, do hurry up and go.

NIALL. Aren't you going to kiss me goodbye?

MILDRED. (turning NIALL round and pushing him towards the door) You'll miss your train. (she opens the door and pushes him out onto the landing)

NIALL. Just a kiss!

MILDRED. (turning her cheek towards him) Oh hurry up and get it over with then. (NIALL barely kisses her) Now off you go. And GOODBYE. (she closes the door) OH that man.

(GLADYS emerges from the kitchen)

GLADYS. Has he gone?

MILDRED. At last.

GLADYS. My husband was the same. Have you been married long?

MILDRED. Too long.

GLADYS. I know how it is. I left mine.

MILDRED. I wish I had the courage.

GLADYS. I've never regretted it.

MILDRED. (walks towards the window) There he goes. Not even a backward glance. God knows what he gets up to in Liverpool.

GLADYS. Do you care?

MILDRED. He brings back money. (turning) How do you manage?

GLADYS. I work.

MILDRED. Of course.

GLADYS. I'm looking for a job at the moment. The problem is finding one that suits.

MILDRED. It's not easy.

GLADYS. No. Especially for women like us. Who've never had to work. I mean we're not working class.

MILDRED. I'd like to go out to work - only... it's the other people. You can never be certain what they might be thinking - or saying, behind your back.

GLADYS. Or to your face! (pause) I tried laundry work once. It was disgusting. And the women. You should have heard them. I felt quite ashamed. Of course they'd got all their dirty talk from men.

MILDRED. That's to be expected.

GLADYS. What I'd really like to do is embroider. But there's no call for it today. Everything is done by machine. To tell the truth, I like doing everything by hand.

MILDRED. Oh so do I. Leisurely.

GLADYS. At my own pace.

MILDRED. When the mood takes one.

GLADYS. It is so much more satisfying.

MILDRED. And personal.

GLADYS. Yes, it's that. (Pause) I only embroider for myself now.

MILDRED. I'm ashamed to admit I don't sew.

GLADYS. It's easy. I could teach you.

MILDRED. It's not that I lack the talent. When I was a little girl, I was watching my mother machine some curtains when the needle went right through her fingernail. Clean through to the other side of her finger. It was ghastly. And do you know what? She just sat there and said, look what's happened Milly. That's all. Then she turned the handle slowly to withdraw the needle. But she didn't shout out; didn't cry, just sucked her finger and carried on as if nothing had happened. But the needle had gone right through her finger! Bone and all. I mean, it MUST have hurt. I KNOW it hurt! You can't tell me having a needle pushed into you doesn't hurt. GOD, it must have been painful.

GLADYS. In those days it wouldn't have done to have complained. Women had to suffer in silence. Cowed under their man. (Silence)

MILDRED. Do you get on with men? I only ask because you said you said you had left your husband.

GLADYS. He was too possessive. And very jealous. The two major faults of men. Possessiveness and jealousy.

MILDRED. And more besides.

GLADYS. A list as long as your arm. It makes me bloody mad! Why shouldn't we be as independent as they are? Oh no. We have to look upon their affairs as mis-adventures. Who doesn't know a man who hasn't gone running back to his wife expecting her to forgive him? He'll stomach a mild scolding but he mustn't be told he's weak and got taken in by some scheming madam. Oh no. But just let him catch you smiling at another man and before you know it you're being told you're the dirtiest old whore living, AND a good deal more besides. Yet he can twist his head off looking after a mini skirt and we're meant to be highly amused and think there's life in the old dog yet. It makes me furious. We're expected to take them back after THEIR affairs have folded... But what happens when a woman comes traipsing back after HER disaster? Eh?

MILDRED. A beating.

GLADYS. Nothing but abuse. Then, as likely as not, you spend the rest of your life being stared at over the top of a newspaper by a man with murder in his eyes. Independence? HA! Equality? Not in our life-time.

MILDRED. It must come one day.

GLADYS. Bound to. But not as long as men continue to believe a woman's affair is the same as his. A man thinks he has to PROVE himself. He wants variety, adventure. A woman's not like that. She wants appreciation. Love.

MILDRED. Are you divorced, Gladys?

GLADYS. Oh no. And I won't. But my brother's divorced. Now there's a man. My brother.

MILDRED. Cleopatra married her brother.

GLADYS. Kind, considerate. What a nice man he turned out to be.

MILDRED. The children of incestuous marriages have thin skulls. Did you know?

GLADYS. But he went and married this dreadful woman.

MILDRED. And they go mad.

GLADYS. You would have liked my brother. And SO good-looking. He's in Canada now, more's the pity. Have you a brother Mildred?

MILDRED. (knocks something over nervously) No! I wouldn't want a brother - But so many girls do. HAVE brothers, I mean.

GLADYS. (curiously suspicious) Y-e-s.

MILDRED. (brightly) Have you ever had an affair, Gladys?

GLADYS. No. Never. And I won't.

MILDRED. But your husband did.

GLADYS. And now! Edgar went sniffing after every little runt in the neighbourhood, like a dog. I half expected him to cock his leg at every lamp post.

MILDRED. I don't think Niall's like that. I doubt if he's ever looked at another woman. Sometimes I wish he would, then perhaps he wouldn't be so, so over-whelming. Possessive.

GLADYS. Is he jealous by nature?

MILDRED. Intolerably so.

GLADYS. What did I tell you.

MILDRED. But I've known women who were jealous.

GLADYS. Ah, but it's different. A woman's realistic

60

when she's jealous. A man isn't. His mind's stuffed full of sexual images and it blinds him. Find a man who's not jealous and you've found a saint.

MILDRED. How does one set about finding a saint?

GLADYS. You won't find him here, that's for sure. Why don't you leave him?

MILDRED. I couldn't.

GLADYS. But you've thought about it.

MILDRED. Often.

GLADYS. What prevents you then?

MILDRED. Where could I go?

GLADYS. To friends. Relations. You must know someone who'd help you.

MILDRED. There's no one.

GLADYS. Haven't you got a sister or a brother...
(MILDRED colours rapidly and is disturbed) Of course, you haven't got a brother. An aunt then?

MILDRED. None. No. No. No one.

GLADYS. That makes it more difficult. That and having no money. (MILDRED is unaware of GLADYS's side-long glance) You haven't any money - have you? (MILDRED stares into space) Perhaps Niall won't come back.

MILDRED. Oh, he always does.

GLADYS. I don't know what you can do then. Unless... You could refuse to open the door to him. Lock him out. Tell him to bugger off.

MILDRED. He'd break the door down - thinking I'd got a man in here.

GLADYS. Then you've no alternative but to pack your bags and go.

MILDRED. I couldn't leave.

GLADYS. But why?

MILDRED. Because... it sounds so silly but - well, this flat's become... I mean, this room. It's a sort of an extension of myself. D'you know what I mean? I'd be lost outside of it.

GLADYS. (sighing) I can understand you becoming attached to a place.

(Silence)

How would it be if we had decided to set up house together and there wasn't any room for him.

MILDRED. (brightening) But you wouldn't want to live here would you? With me?

GLADYS. Why not? I like you. Besides, I've nowhere else to go.

MILDRED. I must say the idea of NOT having a man about the place appeals to me. I don't get on very well with men. I'm not even sure if I LIKE men.

GLADYS. Men are pigs.

MILDRED. Other women seem to cope.

GLADYS. Oh no. No my dear. They've been forced to accept - we all have. We are dominated by them. Seduced, perverted. We're daft. Believe me - I know. Why else do we do the things THEY want us to do? It wouldn't occur to us if we hadn't been... (GLADYS searches for a word - rubbing the top of her forefinger and thumb together)...manipulated.

MILDRED. But I don't get on with women either. I
don't include you. It's those women who appear so
confident I don't like. They're like some beastly
kitten licking the cream off her whiskers. As if she
swallowed a secret elixir and thinking you a fool for
not liking it also. And they look down on you. Like
superior beings. I hate them. Damned bitches.

GLADYS. I keep telling you... Men made them like
that...do this, do that, do the other. Every time I
see a fur coat I think, HA, there goes another one
who gave in and did her nut. O yes. Men have us by
the short hairs - and-don't-they-know it. There's
no need to look so offended. You don't know the half
of it.

MILDRED. All I know is that I can't break out of myself.
I'm not aware of my limits. I want to stretch, but
can't. D'you understand? I thought I would be able
to... I nearly did, once. Some time ago. I thought
I glimpsed what I was capable of being. But it all
went wrong.

GLADYS. Another man?

MILDRED. Niall said he was old enough to be my father.
Nothing happened between us you understand. Nothing
that I'm ashamed of. Nothing coarse or vulgar.
Niall wouldn't believe me of course and accused me of
all sorts of things.

GLADYS. This man - was he married?

MILDRED. Yes.

GLADYS. (sighing) They always are.

MILDRED. He'd no more think of divorcing his wife
than cut off his...

GLADYS. They never will.

MILDRED. So what was the point? The whole thing was over before it had begun. I mean... I wanted more than just... well, **THAT**!

GLADYS. But he didn't.

MILDRED. Old as he was, I had to fight him off. Then... Oh, it was all so sordid. Afterwards...

GLADYS. Afterwards? I thought you said nothing happened.

MILDRED. Well, hardly. It was so brief. Pointless. The same old thing all over again. I hoped it would have been different. You know. Love.

GLADYS. (not at all convinced) Yes. Well. What about my idea of staying here? It's worth a try, isn't it? If it doesn't work out I can be gone before Niall returns. What d'you say?

MILDRED. I don't see why not. There can't be any HARM in it.

GLADYS. Good. That's settled then. You realise I'm broke of course.

MILDRED. Oh, don't worry about that. I've got some money.

GLADYS. Have you?

MILDRED. Yes. Niall knows nothing about it. (for the first time GLADYS relaxes, smiling at MILDRED benignly. MILDRED laughs) I seem to be telling you all my secrets. (excited) I want to show you something... (MILDRED goes to the covered cabinet, removes the shawl and takes out a black book) My diary.

GLADYS. (who has walked over and is looking into the open cabinet, puts her hand inside and withdraws a package of postcards secured by an elastic band) What are these? May I?

64

MILDRED. Please do. (MILDRED removes some other things from the cabinet and carries them to the bed where she sits)

GLADYS. (removing the elastic band as she sits on the bed next to MILDRED) What on earth?...

MILDRED. Post-cards. They're rather...

GLADYS. Disgusting. All bottoms and bosoms. And the captions! Really!

MILDRED. I keep them as a record of how many times Niall's been away.

GLADYS. Of course, you wouldn't have to keep them, if he never came back.

MILDRED. He always comes back.

GLADYS. He might go off with another woman.

MILDRED. No. He loves me.

GLADYS. You seem very certain.

MILDRED. He'd be too embarrassed to ask another woman to tie his tie for him.

GLADYS. That's hardly important.

MILDRED. To Niall it's everything!

GLADYS. What's this? (she takes a box and opens it) Oh!

MILDRED. My jewels.

GLADYS. How pretty. Did Niall give them to you?

MILDRED. Good gracious no. He thinks they're rubbish. That's why I never wear them. Unless I'm alone.

GLADYS. But so pretty. Especially this. (she takes out a necklace)

MILDRED. I'm so glad you like it. That's my favourite.

GLADYS. Won't you put it on - just for me?

MILDRED. All right. (puts it on)

GLADYS. Oh it DOES look pretty. It matches your eyes. (MILDRED gets up off the bed and goes to the mirror) Doesn't it? It's EVER-so pretty. (MILDRED reaches behind her neck to remove it) Oh NO. Don't take it off, Milly. Leave it on. It makes you look ... lovely. There's only me to see. - Niall won't know.

MILDRED. Yes! Why not! Damn Niall! (she walks to the bed and sits down)

GLADYS. If he never came back you could wear them all the time. (she lifts the jewellery out of the box and allows them to fall through her fingers)

MILDRED. I do when he's not here. Once, I put them ALL on.

GLADYS. But he's coming back.

MILDRED. Well - who knows... he might get run over by a bus. (patting the necklace) My father never let me wear jewellery. But he made me have my ears pierced. I kicked up hell I remember. I fought like a cat. This man, he wasn't a doctor. He did it. He used a pin. What I remember is the sound of the needle coming out of the cork.

GLADYS. Cork?

MILDRED. Yes. He put a cork behind my ear so that the needle wouldn't stick into my neck. AND THE SOUND OF IT GOING IN - OR COMING OUT, IT WAS DREADFUL! And then there was the difficulty of

66

keeping the hole open. I had to wear sleepers and twist them round to break the scab which formed. I was nearly sick.

GLADYS. My husband begged me to have mine done.

MILDRED. Be glad you didn't. <u>I let the holes close up</u> <u>when I married Niall.</u> (feeling her ears in turn) I can only just feel a lump where the needle went in.

(Silence)

GLADYS. (picking up a sheaf of untidy papers) Did you do these watercolours? (she begins to leaf through them)

MILDRED. Yes. When I was at school. It was about the only thing I was good at. Art.

GLADYS. Do you still like ELEPHANTS?

MILDRED. Not any more.

GLADYS. (counting the watercolours) There are, one. Two. Three. Four, five. On each one you have scribbled out the face of a person.

MILDRED. I was only a child.

GLADYS. It looks like a boy. Is it a boy? (showing a watercolour to MILDRED who looks away)

MILDRED. I don't know why I keep them - they're rubbish.

GLADYS. And this photograph... (before MILDRED can stop her GLADYS has turned the photograph over) Cecil Wringe. Aged fourteen. Is he your brother?

MILDRED. (confused and reaching out to take the photograph) Yes. I mean - no.

GLADYS. (still reading) West Bromwich. Nineteen

67

Thirty-eight. You lived in West Bromwich?

MILDRED. Yes.

GLADYS. But you didn't have a brother.

MILDRED. Yes.

GLADYS. You mean - yes, you had a brother.

MILDRED. No. He died.

GLADYS. But you DID have a brother?

MILDRED. I don't remember him.

GLADYS. He died?

MILDRED. Of something terrible - yes.

GLADYS. How awful.

MILDRED. We were all so ashamed.

GLADYS. I can imagine.

MILDRED. He went mad.

GLADYS. Did he?

MILDRED. Father warned us it might happen. He said
he knew of hundreds of children who'd gone mad.
He locked Cecil in the cupboard. The cupboard was
the only place where no-one would think of looking.
I discovered him first and knew why he was there
because I used to watch him going mad. I thought it
was infectious and remembered all the times we'd
touched each other. (she shudders) We were made
to feel so ashamed.

GLADYS. Your father was to blame for that.

MILDRED. Oh no. No. I don't blame father. I blame

Cecil.

GLADYS. But he was the victim...

MILDRED. (snatching the photograph) He was horrible.
(and she tears the photograph) Horrible. (and
throws the pieces on the floor) And NIALL'S NO
DIFFERENT.

GLADYS. It's easy to tear up a photograph.

MILDRED. (after considering GLADYS's remark) We'll
deal with him when the time comes. (standing up and
putting her hands on her hips, she surveys the room)
And in the morning we'll go and see how much I've
got in the Post Office.

GLADYS. And draw it out?

MILDRED. We'll spend it. Shall we? Are you game?

GLADYS. I'm game for anything.

ACT TWO

Scene One

(The same room, five days later. It is half past
twelve in the morning.

The brown paper has been removed from the window
and frothy net curtains 'artistically' draped across;
partially obscuring the view through the highly po-
lished glass panes. Over the top of the window is a
deep, red pelmet from which hang two, similarly
coloured curtains drawn well back to allow the
maximum of sunlight to stream into the room.

The door on the wardrobe has been removed and a
red curtain hung across the width of the wardrobe.
MILDRED and NIALL's bed has been made up and is
covered by a counterpane matching the red curtains.
To the right of this bed is another, smaller one,
pushed up against the wall. It too has a red coverlet.

The legs of the cabinet have been utilised as the base
of a table - the top being formed by resting the wardrobe door across it. It stands in the middle of the
room covered by a neatly ironed, crisp, white table
cloth. Facing each other at the end of this table,
their seats pushed tidily under it, are two, simple
wooden chairs. The armchair is propped up straight
and a piece of material draped over it to hide the
shabby upholstery. Some knitting lies on the seat.

The shawl, which once covered the glass cabinet, has been draped and tacked on one of the bare walls.

The room has been swept and tidied, the books hidden - or destroyed, the mirror set straight within its frame and given a coat of gold paint and a cheap, red shade attached to the light flex.

GLADYS, resplendent in her powder blue suit which makes her blonde hair even paler, is setting the table for lunch. It is very quiet within the flat as she fusses round the table. Suddenly, the handle of the door leading out onto the landing is rattled. GLADYS looks up expectantly and lays down the cutlery she is holding. She begins to walk towards the door but stops when a foot kicks the bottom and the handle is rattled again.

She waits.

A fist pounds the door)

NIALL. Open up!

GLADYS. (going cautiously towards the door) Who is it?

NIALL. Me. Open up. (GLADYS hesitates) Come on. I can't stand out here all day.

GLADYS. Who is it?

NIALL. Me. NIALL. Open up. I'm back. (GLADYS slips the catch and opens the door warily. NIALL, minus his tie, pushes past her) Hello. (his voice fades when he sees the changes made to the room. GLADYS closes the door. NIALL, a suitcase in one hand and a small, gaily wrapped parcel in the other, walks about the room looking at the alterations in amazement) WELL. I MUST say... Who'd have believed it? Eh? And CURTAINS. WIDE open. (he humps his suitcase on to MILDRED's bed and fingers the coverlet) Proper swanky. AND another bed! And the wardrobe! Well, well, well. (GLADYS removes his suitcase from the bed and

stands it on the floor) She HAS pulled herself
together, hasn't she? (he drops the parcel on to the
bed, and hands on hips surveys the room again.
GLADYS removes his parcel and balances it on top
of his suitcase. NIALL walks towards the kitchen
door) Any more changes? (he peers into the
kitchen) Goodness - CLEAN. You HAVE been busy
the both of you. Almost Homes and Gardens. And
the bathroom? (NIALL opens the door and looks in)
Ho, ho. (he turns) Couldn't move the mirrors?
(GLADYS, hovering near the table, picks up the
cutlery she had laid down) Still, never mind. Where
is she? Mmm? Don't tell me she's out shopping!

GLADYS. Yes.

NIALL. Wonders will never cease. Good for you Glad.
(he slaps her bottom as he passes. GLADYS goes
rigid and glares at him) How d'you do it? Kindness? Or did you have to take the stick to her? (he
flings himself down on the bed) Marvellous!
(GLADYS looks disapprovingly at NIALL's shoes on
the counterpane. She turns away and walks into the
kitchen) You know Glad, it needed someone like
you. It wasn't any good my trying. I was patient
with her, mind. VERY patient. Perhaps too
tolerant. Weak even. I always gave in to her.
Never wanted to hurt her feelings. I suppose I
always took the easiest way out of any tricky
situation - for her sake. But it never worked. I
couldn't... (NIALL makes a turning movement with
his hand as GLADYS re-enters carrying a jug of
water) Break through. Unlock her, you might say.
I should have realised long ago that only another
woman would be able to penetrate her workings.
Funny though. She hates women. Obviously not
you. Let's hope it lasts. (he sits up) You must
come and visit us. As often as you can. Especially
at first.

(GLADYS walks into the kitchen)

It would do her the world of good to know she had a

friend close by. Her change of heart might become
permanent and who knows - I might even get a
regular job again. Fancy. Work. Every day.
That'd be strange. D'you know - I used to like work.
No. That's not true. It was my way of staying in
bed all day - like Mildred does - or did. A retreat
almost. I felt safe. I knew what was expected of me
at work. I was a draughtsman. A big engineering
firm it was. Well paid too. Life wasn't bad. Then
Mildred took to 'phoning me up - saying she wasn't
well, or lonely and would I come home. It got so
that I was home more often than I was at work.
Naturally I got the boot. Then I took a job in a
shipping office so I'd always be on the end of a
telephone - hoping the firm wouldn't notice the
incoming calls from Mildred. But they soon twigged
on to what was happening, and that was the end of
that. I tried several other jobs, but it was always the
same. No sooner had I arrived at the office than
she'd ring. Would I come home? I wouldn't have
minded if she'd been really ill. But no. She was as
well as you or I. (GLADYS returns with the salt
and pepper and puts them on the table) I wouldn't
have minded if she'd have been all sexed up and I
could have been of some use.

(GLADYS exits)

But she's not like that. So. In the end, I just stayed
home. (he lays back) THAT didn't please her
either. She just climbed into bed and stayed there,
reading her books. Either that or mooned about the
place yawning and saying how tired she felt. I did
all the housework - what there was of it, AND all the
shopping.

(GLADYS re-enters with two glasses)

Everyone - the few friends I had left by then that
is - the ones that dared or bothered to come, well,
they thought I was mad. They didn't understand that
I loved her. I did. I DO. Very much. They thought
I was nuts and ought to get the hell out of it and

leave her to stew in her own juice. But I knew. I
had a feeling that somewhere inside that cocoon she'd
spun round herself was a woman I could really love,
if only I could bring her out of herself. And she was
damned attractive too. She still is. Don't you think
so? (GLADYS sniffs) I bet when you first saw her
you thought to yourself -

(GLADYS goes into kitchen)

There's a woman who's let herself go. That's what
you thought. And I bet you thought it was MY fault -
didn't you?

(GLADYS re-enters carrying a loaf of bread)

Well - she was a strange girl when I first met her.

(GLADYS goes back into the kitchen and returns
almost immediately with two battered suitcases tied
with hairy string. She sets them by the door leading
out on to the landing)

She still is. Deep. Not got much to say for herself.

(GLADYS returns to the kitchen)

Not that she isn't chatty at times, but she never
seems to concentrate when there's serious conversation. It's as if she is not with you. You know what
I mean?

(GLADYS re-enters with a bulky brown paper parcel
which she puts on top of the two suitcases)

In the early days she'd get enthusiastic about all
sorts of things. Didn't matter what. Making her
own clothes. Embroidery - that sort of thing.
Tapestry work. Cooking. She was a good cook. Oh,
everything. Not sex though. She'd never get
enthusiastic about that. Not with me. (he smacks
his fist into his open palm) Always as cold as a slab
of marble. But it was there. The feeling for it was

75

there. Still is. She's like a larder stuffed full of
jams and cheeses - but all ice cold from the damp
draught that seems to blow through her. She even
keeps the door locked on herself. Know what I
mean? (GLADYS looks down at NIALL)

GLADYS. Poetic too.

NIALL. Pardon?

GLADYS. You're articulate.

NIALL. (swinging his legs off the bed and sitting up) I'm
not ignorant - but I generally keep my thoughts to
myself so as not to upset her. (he smacks his hands
and rubs them together) It looks as if you've done
the trick though. (he smiles at GLADYS) Let's
hope she's come to her senses - permanently. Now,
where's my money. (he feels for his wallet) What
did we say? Do you remember?

(They both turn at the sound of a key being inserted
and turned in the lock of the landing door)

I'll pay you later Miss Spendlove. Not a word to
Mildred though.

(The door opens and MILDRED enters. She is
dressed in a light coloured suit and is wearing a shirt
and tie. Her hair is well brushed and shiny. She
looks enthusiastic and happy and remarkably
attractive. She closes the door behind her with her
foot)

MILDRED. What a morning! The PEOPLE! Oh it was
marvellous. (she walks to the table) You'll never
guess what I went and bought.

NIALL. Hello love. It's me.

MILDRED. (putting her shopping bag on the table and
deliberately ignoring NIALL) Mussels. I went mad and
bought - guess. Two quarts. TWO!

NIALL. I'm back.

MILDRED. (turning and looking and turning back to
    GLADYS) I didn't know if you liked them but I
    couldn't resist buying them. When I got out of the
    shop I thought, FOOL, supposing Gladys hates them!
    Do you? Say no.

GLADYS. I adore them. Especially with garlic butter.
    Delicious.

MILDRED. (unpacking her shopping bag) Oh I'm so glad.
    We really ought to eat them with brown bread.

GLADYS. And stout.

MILDRED. Wouldn't that be marvellous. We could do
    that tonight. I'll get the bread and the stout this
    afternoon. And tonight we'll make pigs of ourselves.

NIALL. Hey! Can't you see? I'm back. Don't I get a
    welcome? (he walks up to MILDRED and puts his arm
    round her shoulder. MILDRED shrugs it off)

MILDRED. Not now. (to GLADYS) Am I awfully late?
    (as they walk towards the kitchen together...) I saw
    a most marvellous dress in Stanhopes. (from the
    kitchen) You must come with me and tell me what you
    think of it.

GLADYS. Let's have lunch first. It's all ready.

NIALL. (walking up to the kitchen door) It smells good.
    And am I starving?

MILDRED. (pushing past him) Mmm?

NIALL. I haven't eaten since last night. Just a cup of
    tea on the train this morning.

MILDRED. More fool you then.

NIALL. Know what today is?

MILDRED. Friday.

NIALL. I KNOW it's Friday.

MILDRED. Then why ask?

NIALL. But it's something else as well.

MILDRED. (to GLADYS who enters carrying a steaming
saucepan filled with soup) That dress is yellow.
Bright yellow. Do you think yellow will suit me?

GLADYS. (setting down the saucepan) Why not? With
your dark hair it should look ravishing.

NIALL. You HAVE forgotten what today is, haven't you?

MILDRED. (sitting down at the table) I've told you. It's
Friday.

NIALL. Yes, but not just any Friday.

MILDRED. Oh do shut up. It's Friday. For Gladys a
meatless day. A fish day. She's a Catholic. (she
smiles at GLADYS)

NIALL. Alright. So Friday's a fish day. But it's also
your birthday. Had you forgotten?

MILDRED. (groaning) Why in heaven's name do you have
to go and remind me it's my birthday!

NIALL. AH HA! I've bought you something. (he goes
and fetches the brightly wrapped parcel) A present.
(he holds it out to her) Many Happy Returns of the
day darling. (he leans forward to kiss her. MIL-
DRED ducks the kiss)

MILDRED. After lunch.

NIALL. It's a Birthday present.

MILDRED. AFTER lunch. (NIALL throws the parcel

on to the bed and tries to catch GLADYS's eye, but
she bends her head over the saucepan)

NIALL. I suppose if I'd forgotten it was your birthday
you wouldn't have given me a moment's peace.

MILDRED. (holding out her bowl for GLADYS to fill
with soup) Not too much. (GLADYS begins to
ladle the soup) I've suddenly gone off my food.
(GLADYS looks out of the corner of her eye at
NIALL)

NIALL. Where am I to sit?

(GLADYS, having finished ladling, sits down and
picks up a spoon)

Where's mine?

MILDRED. Your what?

NIALL. Whatever it is you're having. Or aren't I
included in this cosy little lunch.

(Silence)

Well - am I?

MILDRED. No.

NIALL. I beg your pardon?

MILDRED. No. What's happened to your tie?

NIALL. Eh? Oh. I undid it without thinking. (He
produces it from his pocket. GLADYS, unable to
control a giggle has to rush into the kitchen with a
mouthful of soup) What's got into her?

MILDRED. Gladys has a highly developed sense of the absurd.

NIALL. That's going to make for difficulties.

MILDRED. Oh? I don't see why. I find it rather refreshing.

NIALL. It will become irritating after a while.

MILDRED. I fail to see why it should concern you. The three of us aren't going to live together.

NIALL. Thank God for that. (GLADYS returns)

GLADYS. I'm sorry. (she sits but immediately begins to giggle again. Her giggle is infectious and MILDRED starts to snigger)

NIALL. Am I to share the joke?

MILDRED. You are the joke.

NIALL. (visibly disturbed) What are you two up to?

MILDRED. We're not UP to anything.

NIALL. You're suddenly both very close. I go away - I've hardly turned my back - and what do I find?

MILDRED. What do you find?

NIALL. I'm not sure. It's as if I've been... well - dismissed.

MILDRED. You have. You'll find everything there. (she points to the two suitcases and the parcel) All your clothes. Everything.

NIALL. (glancing at the suitcases and then at the two women) What ARE you talking about. MY things?

GLADYS. Mildred has decided that she doesn't want to

live with you anymore. She is asking you to leave.

NIALL. JUST like that? Mmmm? And where, may I
ask, do YOU fit into all this, eh? Why can't
Mildred speak for herself?

MILDRED. Gladys has got nothing to do with my decision.

NIALL. Oh. YOU decided, did you?

MILDRED. Yes.

NIALL. Without any prompting from her?

MILDRED. Yes.

NIALL. I see. And I don't have any say in the matter?

MILDRED. No. You see Niall....How can I put it? Living
with you - I always felt restricted. Hemmed in.
Enclosed. Like a flower which never opened. I
wanted to blossom, but couldn't. I can't - not with
you around. I'm sure you understand. You - were -
always - SO - understanding.

NIALL. Apparently not. But where does SHE come into
all this?

(Silence)

Well come on. I might as well know the truth.

(Silence)

Have neither of you got anything to say?

(to GLADYS) What about you Miss Spendlove?

GLADYS. What do you want me to say?

NIALL. WHAT HAVE YOU BEEN DOING TO MY WIFE?

GLADYS. Doing? Nothing. (to MILDRED) Have I?

(MILDRED shakes her head and hunches her shoulders) You see?

NIALL. This is a conspiracy. (to GLADYS) I suppose I'm to go because you are staying? Is that it? You now have pride of place in Mildred's affections. Having successfully wormed your way into the apple, you're determined to stay until the apple rots and disintegrates? (MILDRED and GLADYS pull faces) Is that it?

You couple of bloody...

To think - that MY wife...

MILDRED. Your wife what?

NIALL. (to GLADYS) I suppose she's wallowing in YOUR bathwater now. (GLADYS frowns and MILDRED groans)

GLADYS. Bathwater?

NIALL. Enjoying you second-hand is she?

MILDRED. You're being absurd Niall. If you're going to get all emotional, then you'd better leave. (rising) Go on. There are your things. Take them. And don't come back.

And don't forget your little parcel.

NIALL. I - AM - NOT - LEAVING! And that's your present.

MILDRED. My birthday present (she picks it up) And what did the thoughtful little man bring me all the way back from Liverpool? Mmmm. (she tears open the gaily wrapped package and pulls out a long, white, simple nightdress) What is it?

NIALL. A nightdress.

MILDRED. (to GLADYS) Mister Scringeour's bought me
    a nightdress.

GLADYS. Fancy!

MILDRED. (holding the nightdress up to herself) What
    d'you think? Do I look G-L-A-M-O-R-O-U-S?

GLADYS. Gorgeous!

MILDRED. Do I? (to NIALL) Does it make me
    I-R-R-E-S-I-S-T-I-B-L-E?

GLADYS. (trying to suppress her laughter) Bewitching!

MILDRED. (still addressing NIALL) A-L-L-U-R-I-N-G?
    (turning round and round) S-E-D-U-C-T-I-V-E? Is
    your heart beginning to beat madly? Is it? Do you
    want to take me in your arms? To C-R-U-S-H me
    against your hairy chest in a W-I-L-D embrace?
    To touch me. To feel me Y-I-E-L-D-I-N-G! Are
    all your nerve ends quivering with excitement? Your
    knees trembling? Are they? Do you feel you want
    to T-E-A-R this negligee from me and bury your face
    in my flesh? Well? DO YOU? Then why don't you?
    GO ON! TEAR IT INTO SHREDS! (she balls and
    throws the nightdress at NIALL's head) HERE!
    CATCH! (GLADYS rocks backwards and forwards
    with laughter. NIALL picks the nightdress off the
    floor, shakes it, dusts it and folds it up carefully.
    While MILDRED and GLADYS laugh, NIALL tries
    to repack the nightdress in the torn wrapping paper)

    (Her laughter beginning to subside and seated once
    again opposite GLADYS) Why didn't you buy me a
    pair of knickers?

GLADYS. Or a bra?

MILDRED. A G-string!

GLADYS. Suspenders!

(The women burst into laughter again. NIALL, looking at them, slowly draws out his tie from his jacket pocket and turns to the mirror)

MILDRED. Why didn't you buy me a tie Niall? I've taken to wearing ties. Look. (she stands) Do you like my tie? Eh? Well do you? It's just like yours. isn't it Niall? (she flaps the end of it) Nicer than yours. Why didn't you buy me a tie if you wanted to please me?

NIALL. It never occurred to me that you wanted one.

MILDRED. Do you think it odd of me to want to wear a tie?

NIALL. No. (fingering his own tie, he makes his way towards the mirror) I'm only surprised to see how it becomes you. (standing in front of the mirror, he struggles to knot his tie. MILDRED draws GLADYS's attention to NIALL's difficulties and they both try to suppress their giggles. MILDRED suddenly composes her features and approaches NIALL)

MILDRED. Shall I tie it for you?

NIALL. I can manage thank you.

MILDRED. (trying to turn NIALL round) Let me.

NIALL. I'm quite capable, thank you.

MILDRED. But I can tie it so much better than you can. Come on. Let me.

(NIALL turns and faces MILDRED)

(She puts her hands on his shoulders) Sit on the bed. (leading NIALL over) Now keep still. (she takes his tie, turns up NIALL's collar and, holding the tie at either end, puts it over NIALL's head, round his neck and pulls it - so that NIALL has to brace his head)

NIALL. STEADY ON! You'll have my head off. (MILDRED
motionless, gazes down at him) Well hurry up then if
you're going to do it.

MILDRED. I'm sorry. (she puts one end of the tie over
the other, makes a half knot and then, suddenly,
and with a shout, pulls the knot tight; throttling
NIALL. His mouth open, his eyes bulging, he falls
backwards on the bed, struggling to free himself from
the tie which is throttling him) COME ON - I'VE GOT
HIM!

(With a whoop, GLADYS runs across and flings
herself on top of NIALL. Pinned by the two women,
he is helpless. He rolls his head from side to side
and gasps)

GLADYS. Hold on to him! TIGHTER! (NIALL's feet
begin to pedal the air)

MILDRED. Very much tighter?

GLADYS. YES. GO ON. He should turn purple soon.
Go ON!

MILDRED. This tight?

GLADYS. (taking and pulling one end of the tie)
Y-e-e-e-e-s.

(NIALL stops struggling)

MILDRED. Can you hear me Niall? NIALL! Are you
listening? (NIALL nods his head feebly and rolls
his eyes) We'll let you go if you do exactly what we
say. D'you understand? (NIALL nods again) Don't
try and do anything silly. Or else. (she pulls the
tie tighter and NIALL bucks. She then ties a slip
knot in the tie so that she is left with a length of
tie to hold on to. The two women slide off him.
GLADYS backs away while MILDRED holds on to the

end of the tie) Up. UP! (she tugs. NIALL struggles
into a sitting position. His eyes are screwed tight
and he is grimacing. He tries to ease the tie away
from his throat) I warn you'. (MILDRED tugs and
NIALL desists, immediately) NOW. Down on your
knees. (NIALL obeys quickly as MILDRED gives
another tug) Good dog. Let's go walkies. COME
ON! (she kicks NIALL and pulls on the tie. When
they reach the table, she ties the tie to one of the
legs of the table and then sits down. She raises a
warning finger) Now stay. (NIALL sighs and puts up
his hand to his throat. MILDRED slaps his hand) I
said STAY!

NIALL.   (weakly) You nearly strangled me just then.

MILDRED. We'll do that later. When we've finished with
you. Won't we Miss Spendlove?

GLADYS.   We will indeed.

MILDRED.   The tricks first I think.

GLADYS.   But he might not be house trained.

MILDRED.   They never are. (she tugs the tie)

GLADYS.   And you know how excitable little pups get.
They widdle all over the place.

MILDRED.   Especially mongrels. (and she kicks NIALL)
We'll have to get him a dirt box. He can do his
messes in that.

GLADYS.   We'll have to train him. With a stick. Beat
obedience into him.

MILDRED.   No. He might like the whip. Men do, you
know. I mean, dogs do.

GLADYS.   How shall we teach him obedience then?

MILDRED. With kindness?

GLADYS. No. We don't want him gratefully dogging our heels all day. (at the unintended pun, both women laugh) and we don't want to turn him into a lap dog - he'd be wanting to share our bed with us at nights.

MILDRED. Huh! What a disgusting thought! (their indignation is exaggerated)

GLADYS. We ought to train him not to sniff around.

MILDRED. Dirty! Did you hear what Auntie Gladys said doggy? (NIALL runs his hand over his face) And they're always licking. They lick everything! Hugh!

GLADYS. We could cut off his tongue to stop him slobbering.

MILDRED. An excellent idea!

GLADYS. With a pair of scissors.

MILDRED. With a pair of SHARP scissors.

GLADYS. And we could neuter him.

MILDRED. With the scissors. I'm all for that. It would solve a lot of problems. Get the scissors Gladys.

NIALL. Please. A glass of water.

MILDRED. (as GLADYS gets up to fetch the scissors) Unbutton your trousers Niall.

NIALL. Don't be so damned silly.

MILDRED. UNDO YOUR TROUSERS!

GLADYS. Here are the scissors.

NIALL. PLEASE Mildred. May I have a glass of water?

MILDRED. Are you going to get your trousers off...?

GLADYS. Or do we have to cut through them?

NIALL. I want some water.

MILDRED. Hold his legs Gladys... (GLADYS pounces
on NIALL, holds his legs and the three begin to
struggle) Hold still you fool or you'll get cut up the
stomach!

GLADYS. GO ON! QUICKLY! CUT! (NIALL screams
and the women release him)

(NIALL holding his thigh rocks backwards and
forwards clutching his thigh)

MILDRED. (sitting down) Frightened? Were you
frightened?

NIALL. I want a glass of water. (he goes to untie his
tie but MILDRED hits him - with all her strength,
across the back of the head)

MILDRED. Are you frightened? (NIALL is silent) I
said - ARE YOU FRIGHTENED? ANSWER ME! (and
she jabs at him with the scissors)

NIALL. OUCH! For GOD'S SAKE woman - look what
you're doing!

MILDRED. ANSWER ME THEN. ARE YOU FRIGHTENED?

NIALL. ALRIGHT THEN! YES. YES - I'M FRIGH-
TENED!

MILDRED. Say woof.

NIALL. Don't be so damned silly.

MILDRED. (jabbing him with the scissors) BARK!

NIALL. OH FOR GOD'S SAKE - woof. WOOF!

MILDRED. Again.

NIALL. Woof. NOW. Can I have a glass of water.
PLEASE.

MILDRED. LOUDER!

NIALL. CAN I HAVE A GLASS OF...

MILDRED. (hitting him) BARK - you dog!

NIALL. WUF.

MILDRED. Louder.

NIALL. I shall be sick.

MILDRED. LOUDER!

NIALL. I'm going to be sick I tell you.

GLADYS. He looks very pale.

MILDRED. He's lying.

GLADYS. I don't think so.

MILDRED. Are you going to be sick? Oh you poor little
thing. (she kneels down beside him and loosens his
tie) You'd better sit on the bed.

(GLADYS goes into the kitchen and returns with a
glass of water)

GLADYS. Here drink this.

NIALL. Thank you. (he takes and sips from the glass of
water)

(Silence)

MILDRED. Better?

(NIALL swallows, nods and feels his neck)

89

(GLADYS and MILDRED look at one another. NIALL
stands up and puts the glass on the table)

NIALL. We've played some daft games in our time but
that was the maddest. (he clears his throat and
fingers his neck) You had me really frightened for a
moment. I felt certain you intended to kill me.

GLADYS. Perhaps she did.

NIALL. This is insane! Since I've been away something's
happened which I don't understand. It doesn't take an
idiot to put two and two together to know why. It's
HER. (he points to GLADYS)

GLADYS. You invited me to your home.

NIALL. I took pity on you.

GLADYS. Did it never occur to you that it might have
been the other way about? It was YOU who did all the
talking. YOU wanted my sympathy. And help. It was
your Life history I heard. I hardly spoke.

NIALL. You seemed understanding.

GLADYS. Because I listened? I was bored. I was
listening to an old cracked record I had heard so
many times before that I was numb.

NIALL. You said you hadn't a place to go to.

GLADYS. No more I had.

NIALL. So you come here - set up house - turn
Mildred against me...

GLADYS. Don't be so damned ridiculous.

NIALL. ...and tart the place up. (he indicates the
changed room)

GLADYS. That had nothing to do with me. Your wife

bought and arranged everything.

NIALL. I don't believe you. Where did you get the
money?

MILDRED. I had a little. In the Post Office.

NIALL. You never told me.

MILDRED. Why should I? It was my money. It's all
gone now. Almost. There's just enough left to buy a
yellow dress I saw. Then it's all gone.

NIALL. Alright - so you did everything yourself. But why
the sudden decision to kick me out? And why does
SHE have to stay?

MILDRED. I'm sorry Niall. But...I like living with
Gladys. Better than...Well. With you.

NIALL. I should have guessed. I knew there was something queer about the whole set up the minute I
walked in.

MILDRED. What d'you mean - QUEER?

NIALL. You and her. Do I have to spell it out?

MILDRED. I wish you would.

GLADYS. You're quite wrong, you know.

NIALL. Am I?

GLADYS. Ab-so-lutely wrong. I'm staying here because
Mildred likes me as a companion. Someone to talk
to. Someone who she thinks understands her. As you
said earlier, it takes a woman to understand a woman.

NIALL. Well. I could have wished the circumstances of
my demolition to have been different. I would have
preferred a man to have replaced me - not a woman.
It would not have been so humiliating.

(Silence)

MILDRED. I'm sorry Niall.

NIALL. So am I. For the twelve long years that have at
last been reduced to nothing. Nothing. I don't know
how much you know about us Miss Spendlove. How
much my - Mildred has told you. No doubt you've
both been busy with your tongues whilst I've been
away, but I will enlighten you by setting the record
straight.

MILDRED. There's no need for a long oration Niall.
Just say your goodbyes and go.

NIALL. If Mildred told you we were married, she lied.

MILDRED. Will you go!

NIALL. She won't marry me. Ever. Neither will she
submit to the indignity of bearing children. Those
are her own words. Oh, she agreed to live with me.
Yes. Why I don't know, unless she saw in her misery
a kind of Christian Martyrdom. You know - pain and
suffering lead to joy and fulfilment. To marry me
would be to surrender her freedom. To renounce
forever her equality. She's like the limping girl
with the cork boot - deformed but wishing her legs
equal. Not only wishing, but contorting herself to
show that they are, and walking with one leg in the
gutter to prove it. She fights a perpetual war, not
realising she is a casualty of her youth. So she turns
her wrath against ME.

GLADYS. I said you were articulate.

NIALL. Neither of you believe me.

GLADYS. By the time the next generation have grown up,
the only difference between men and women will be
confinement.

MILDRED. And bras.

92

GLADYS. Even that is doubtful.

NIALL. What are you afraid of? That you might be considered only as woman? Is that it? Have you thought that my fear might be that I am not man enough? WELL? You may throw off the absurdities which my sex has imposed upon you. Laws will be changed. Social equality of the sexes established. But what you will NOT be able to alter is the fact that you are women. And you must live out your life as women. The longing to be the prime mover is only a phantasy. Oh, you may mutilate your breasts - have done with them, elongate your clitoris - but you will have changed nothing. Not a thing. All you will have done is to have underlined your own, personal disquiet and added fuel to a frustration which will burn up your lives miserably.

MILDRED. What has all this dirty talk got to do with the last twelve years I'd like to know. (to GLADYS) He's sex mad.

GLADYS. They all are.

NIALL. I admit that the love I first had for Mildred was purely carnal... (MILDRED and GLADYS pull faces)

MILDRED. What did I tell you?

NIALL. ALL love is sexual.

MILDRED. Don't be so disgusting.

GLADYS. All love is self love.

MILDRED. He's just trying to make dirty talk. Love is sex indeed! You don't know what you're talking about!

NIALL. (whose voice slowly rises to a climax) Was it disgusting when your skin became buttermilk and your eyes flashed? When your whole body became alive and nervous? When the only purpose of your life - when whole days, weeks, months were filled

93

with the thoughts of one man - LANGLEY! and when all you could think of was surrounding him with your loving? Well? Was it? Was it disgusting then?

MILDRED. SHUT UP!

NIALL. IF IT WAS DISGUSTING IT WAS BECAUSE OF THAT DAMNED CUPBOARD IN WEST BROMWICH!

MILDRED. I'll kill you... (she runs to NIALL)

NIALL. Don't bother. You already have. Most success-fully.

MILDRED. I wish I had.

NIALL. It only needed this. This final humiliation.

MILDRED. THEN I'M GLAD. D'YOU HEAR? GLAD!

(Silence)

NIALL. I loved you once - like no other being on earth. An hour ago, I still did.

MILDRED. (mockingly) HA HA.

NIALL. Not in the same way I used to. Frustrated love is sublimated into good deeds. I became attentive. Patient.

MILDRED. HO HO.

NIALL. I don't expect you to see it that way at all. Or to realise what you've done to me.

MILDRED. That's it - BLAME ME.

NIALL. I'm not blaming you. It was my own fault. Because I lived in hope - imagining it only needed patience, kindness and time. I didn't realise I was contributing a morbid sickness.

MILDRED. You were just a dirty pig.

NIALL. Yes. A dead porker. Neatly sliced; sandwiched
   and devoured by old brother Hubbard - WHO LIVED
   IN A CUPBOARD!

   (MILDRED throws something)

MILDRED. You're very free with your talk, aren't you?
   It doesn't require much effort to make words -
   and that's all you've ever done - talk. And make
   promises. Yes. To justify your own filth.

NIALL. For twelve years Mildred I've stood by you. Like
   a brother to your sister.

   (MILDRED goes berserk but a sharp push from NIALL
   separates them)

MILDRED. Get out and leave us alone!

NIALL. You don't believe me, do you Miss Spendlove?
   Eh? You think maybe I've been brutal. No. I'm
   almost as mad as she is. Because I've been gentle.

MILDRED. HA!

NIALL. I've urged her to make her own decisions. Stood
   away from her to allow her to expand. Enclosed her
   in my arms when she was afraid. I've stroked and
   massaged her tensions until my consideration was
   exhausted. Given her my shoulder to blot up tears of
   self-pity. I've prodded her into situations she was too
   timid to approach. I've shielded and protected her
   from the animosity of her parents and kept her safe
   in a world she found unendurable.

MILDRED. You did all that? HA!

NIALL. I did more.

MILDRED. Do tell me. I'm curious to know how YOU think we have spent these last twelve years.

NIALL. I spent them growing to love you while I came to hate and despise myself.

MILDRED. HA. HA. FUNNY HA. HA.

NIALL. I would like to think it was a real love, but I suspect my affections were merely a sublimation of all the appetites and desires which were denied me and which I have almost become ashamed of.

MILDRED. Poor little Niall. Frustrated is he?

NIALL. (walking towards the window) YES I AM. Only I'm trying very hard to convince myself that I am not. That I no longer need you that way. (Turning) Like you, I have convinced myself that it is of no consequence whatsoever.

MILDRED. Ho ho ho.

NIALL. So my love has become strangely impersonal. Like bathwater. (MILDRED laughs, but a little too loudly) A substitution. A sort of mystical sexuality in which the more keen my humiliation, the greater my joy.

MILDRED. You waintly little prig.

NIALL. And d'you know? I-no-longer-fear-death.

MILDRED. (clapping her hands) Bravo! Three cheers for bravery. The man's a hero.

NIALL. I did once. Oh yes. (Pointing) SHE knows that. But I've never feared the mortician like she does. His little twists of cotton wool... (MILDRED bounds up off the bed and rushes towards him shouting)...and his outrageous fingers. (He holds MILDRED's

wrists) Your final indignity will be in death. AND YOU
CARE! (MILDRED begins to kick him)

MILDRED. PIG!

NIALL. (trying to ward off MILDRED and hold her
    wrists at the same time) AND I LIVE - MISS
    SPENDLOVE, IN THE CONSTANT SHADOW - OF
    HER MONSTROUS SYMBOLIC REJECTION -
    DENIAL - AND NIHILATION OF HER... (MILDRED
    manages to wrestle free one of her hands and to
    strike NIALL repeatedly about the face and mouth.
    Screaming and shouting, she struggles with him until
    NIALL, getting a firm grip on her shoulders, begins
    to shake her violently. With a final push NIALL
    sends MILDRED sprawling on to the bed. MILDRED
    cries hysterically and kicks her feet in rage. NIALL
    turns to GLADYS)

    Do I comfort her or do you?

    I think perhaps you'd better. I'm suddenly exhausted.

    (GLADYS crosses to the bed and looks down at
    MILDRED. Then GLADYS sits down on the bed and
    begins to stroke MILDRED's hair)

    (Silence)

    (He walks towards the bathroom door)

    Stay with her. She'll need you. You or somebody
    else.

    (He enters the bathroom and shuts the door)

    (MILDRED continues to sob. GLADYS lets her gaze
    wander round the room. It is as if for the first time
    she is assessing the improbability of staying. She
    sighs and turns to MILDRED)

GLADYS. Come on Miss Wringe. Pull yourself together.
    Crying's not going to solve anything. Not now, or

97

ever. Dry your eyes.

MILDRED. (into her hands. Between sobs) He's always saying things like that to me.

GLADYS. Like what?

MILDRED. You heard him. I can't help the way I am. I didn't always used to be like this.

GLADYS. We all change sooner or later.

MILDRED. I was a nice girl.

GLADYS. Who of us weren't?

MILDRED. Life was going to be so different. I didn't want it to turn out like this.

GLADYS. (a trifle bored) Of course you didn't.

MILDRED. It's HIM.

GLADYS. He sounded reasonable.

MILDRED. How can you say that!

And stop messing my hair about!!!

(GLADYS withdraws her hand as if burnt and her face becomes set) How can you possibly say that? You heard what he said. Why didn't you stand up for me?

GLADYS. I've a train to catch. (she stands up. MILD-RED's mouth drops open)

MILDRED. You what?

GLADYS. I shall want some money.

MILDRED. You're not going to leave me...? Gladys! You can't go - just like that.

GLADYS. (looking for her coat) I must. Have you got any money?

(MILDRED, dazed, gets to her feet, and as if in a dream, picks up her handbag)

MILDRED. But we agreed... (opening her handbag and scrabbling about inside but keeping her eyes on GLADYS) You said you'd stay with me. Wanted to stay.

GLADYS. Nothing definite was agreed.

(Getting into her coat)

MILDRED. But I bought the bed for you Gladys. I - I did all this... all this - just for you.

GLADYS. How much?

MILDRED. How much what?

GLADYS. Money!

MILDRED. WHAT D'YOU KEEP ON ABOUT MONEY FOR? I'M ASKING YOU TO STAY. TO LIVE WITH ME.

GLADYS. What about the money for the yellow dress you said you were going to buy? Where's that?

MILDRED. GLADYS! Didn't you hear? I WANT you to stay! These last five days have been the happiest in my life. Weren't you happy?

GLADYS. (extending her hand and snapping her fingers) Come on. LOOK.

MILDRED. You said you were. You said for once it had worked. For the two of us. We WERE happy.

GLADYS. Do I have to snatch? Give.

MILDRED. Oh TAKE IT! (she throws the handbag at

GLADYS who fails to catch it. GLADYS picks the
handbag up and rummages through the contents) Oh
GLADYS, why won't you tell me what's wrong? What
have I done? Is it something I've said?

GLADYS. Three bloody pounds. Is that all?

MILDRED. No. I mean YES. GLADYS you can't just
walk out on me. Not without an explanation. It'll be
different when Niall's gone. You'll see. I'll do
anything you want. Anything. But don't leave. Please.

GLADYS. (throwing the handbag into the chair, stuffing
the money into her pocket and looking about her) You
can get this back off Niall. He owes me anyhow.

MILDRED. Owes you? Owes you what?

GLADYS. Money. (she withdraws the notes from her
pocket and holds them up) Money, for coming here.
(GLADYS puts a few odds and ends in her case and then
pulls on her gloves)

MILDRED. It's HIM, isn't it? It's Niall?

(She seizes hold of GLADYS's coat)

GLADYS. Stop it! (she frees herself from MILDRED's
grip) And pull yourself together.

MILDRED. (grasping hold of GLADYS's coat again) BUT
HE'S GOING. HE WON'T BE HERE. JUST THE TWO
OF US!

GLADYS. WILL - YOU - LEAVE - GO! (and she slaps
MILDRED)

(Silence)

MILDRED. You HIT ME! No one's ever hit me. WHY?
WHAT HAVE I DONE?

GLADYS. Done? NOTHING. It's what you might do. To

me. To everyone. Now. Let me pass.

MILDRED. I don't understand NO! (as GLADYS tries to push past her)

GLADYS. Out of my way.

MILDRED. I WON'T LET YOU GO. NOT UNTIL YOU TELL ME.

(She puts her back to the door to prevent GLADYS from leaving)

GLADYS. WILL YOU LET ME PASS!

(Unable to control her temper, GLADYS strikes MILDRED, turns her and pushes her backwards. MILDRED screams. GLADYS slaps MILDRED's face again) And that's from NIALL. (she opens the door)

(As she backs out of the door) AND GOOD RIDDANCE!

(She turns but turns back and points)

AND YOU WANT TO GET RID OF THOSE CURTAINS. THEY MAKE THE PLACE LOOK LIKE A TART'S BOUDOIR!

(She slams the door)

MILDRED. I HATE YOU, I HATE YOU! (she runs to the door and drags it wide open) I HATE YOU. GLADYS? D'YOU HEAR? I HATE YOU!

(She turns and runs to the window. Opening it, she leans out; waiting for GLADYS to appear)

I HATE YOU!

YOU FAT OLD BAG. I HATE YOU.

D'YOU HEAR ME GLADYS - I HATE YOU!

(NIALL opens the bathroom door)

GLADYS!

DON'T PRETEND YOU CAN'T HEAR ME!

I HATE YOU!

(She leans out even further)

GLADYS!

(NIALL tiptoes towards MILDRED)

I KNOW YOU CAN HEAR ME.

I HATE YOU. HATE YOU!

(NIALL, coming up behind MILDRED, puts his hands on her bottom and pushes her. MILDRED gives a startled cry and disappears out of the window, screaming. After the sound, as of a body landing on empty dustbins, there is silence. NIALL walks to the mirror and begins to tie his tie. While he struggles to remember which end to cross over which, the door slowly opens and GLADYS enters)

GLADYS. You pushed her.

NIALL. You saw her fall.

GLADYS. I saw you push her.

NIALL. The window sill is very low.

GLADYS. I saw her fall after you'd pushed her out.

NIALL. She must have tripped and fallen.

GLADYS. She somersaulted on to her head.

NIALL. Or she could have jumped.

GLADYS. She fell against the dustbin in the basement area. Onto the concrete.

NIALL. I'd like to think it was an accident.

GLADYS. I saw your hands upturned as you pushed her out.

NIALL. I was in the bathroom at the time.

GLADYS. You stood behind her with your tie undone.

(NIALL tries to tie his tie quickly, and fails)

NIALL. She was leaning out too far.

GLADYS. You were in the bathroom when it happened.

NIALL. I shouted at her to be careful...

GLADYS. You'd gone to tie your tie.

NIALL. ... I made to save her.

GLADYS. You heard a scream...

NIALL. It might have looked as if I was pushing her.

GLADYS. You dashed into here...

NIALL. She was falling before I reached her.

GLADYS. And she was gone.

NIALL. I couldn't bring myself to look.

GLADYS. I came up to break the sad news. Your wife is dead.

NIALL. Poor, poor Mildred.

GLADYS. It is the living who need our sympathy.

NIALL. You are a great comfort Gladys.

GLADYS. In a time of crisis, it is the strong who
inherit.

NIALL. There are many who wouldn't be so understanding.

GLADYS. I shall expect you to remove the mirrors from
the bathroom.

NIALL. I'd forgotten it is customary to drape the mirrors
in a house of death.

GLADYS. And to sleep in the single bed.

NIALL. I will have the Council lay straw outside the
house.

GLADYS. And we will change the curtains.

NIALL. I will buy a yard of black crepe to wind round
the lamp-post and each other's arms.

GLADYS. We'll have a good strong blind.

NIALL. You are so practical.

GLADYS. The wishes of the dead must be respected by
the living.

NIALL. Life is a continuous cycle.

GLADYS. The police must be informed.

NIALL. That's a man's job.

GLADYS. ...and the mortician. There are things to
be done.

NIALL. I will lay out her body myself.

GLADYS. That is woman's work.

It is your duty to inform the police.

NIALL. I'll go right away. (moving towards the door)

GLADYS. You're minus your tie.

NIALL. It doesn't matter.

GLADYS. What will people think if they see you without a tie? Come here.

NIALL. You'll tie it for me?

GLADYS. Of course. Come here. (NIALL approaches her) Kneel.

NIALL. Yes?

GLADYS. I said kneel.

Don't be obstinate. We have our whole lives before us.

NIALL. I'd rather not.

GLADYS. KNEEL!

NIALL. Just this once then. (and he slowly sinks to his knees)

GLADYS. (beginning to tie his tie) Once is enough. Hold your head up.

(As NIALL puts back his head, tears are seen to run from his eyes)

C AND B PLAYSCRIPTS

		Cloth	Paper
*PS 1	TOM PAINE by Paul Foster	21s	9s
*PS 2	BALLS and other plays (The Recluse, Hurrah for the Bridge, The Hessian Corporal) by Paul Foster	25s	10s
PS 3	THREE PLAYS (Lunchtime Concert, Coda, The Inhabitants) by Olwen Wymark	21s	7s
*PS 4	CLEARWAY by Vivienne C. Welburn	21s	7s
*PS 5	JOHNNY SO LONG and THE DRAG by Vivienne C. Welburn	25s	8s
*PS 6	SAINT HONEY and OH DAVID, ARE YOU THERE? by Paul Ritchie	25s	11s
PS 7	WHY BOURNEMOUTH? and other plays (The Missing Links, An Apple a Day) by John Antrobus	25s	10s
*PS 8	THE CARD INDEX and other plays (Gone Out, The Interrupted Act) by Tadeusz Rozewicz trans. Adam Czerniawski	25s	11s
PS 9	US by Peter Brook and others	42s	25s
*PS 10	SILENCE and THE LIE by Nathalie Sarraute trans. Maria Jolas	25s	9s

		Cloth	Paper
PS 30	THE LUNATIC, THE SECRET SPORTSMAN AND THE WOMEN NEXT DOOR and VIBRATIONS by Stanley Eveling	30s	12s
*PS 31	STRINDBERG by Colin Wilson	21s	9s
*PS 32	THE FOUR LITTLE GIRLS Pablo Picasso trans. Roland Penrose	25s	10s
PS 33	MACRUNE'S GUEVARA by John Spurling	25s	9s
*PS 34	THE MARRIAGE Witold Gombrowicz trans. Louis Iribarne	35s	15s
*PS 35	BLACK OPERA and THE GIRL WHO BARKS LIKE A DOG by Gabriel Cousin trans. Irving F. Lycett	30s	15s
*PS 36	SAWNEY BEAN by Robert Nye and Bill Watson	25s	10s
PS 37	COME AND BE KILLED and DEAR JANET ROSENBERG, DEAR MR. KOONING by Stanley Eveling	35s	15s
PS 38	DISCOURSE ON VIETNAM by Peter Weiss trans. Geoffrey Skelton	38s	18s
*PS 39	! HEIMSKRINGLA ! or THE STONED ANGELS by Paul Foster	30s	12s

		Cloth	Paper
*PS 41	THE HOUSE OF BONES by Roland Dubillard trans. Barbara Wright	35s	15s
*PS 42	THE TREADWHEEL and COIL WITHOUT DREAMS by Vivienne C. Welburn	30s	15s
PS 43	THE NUNS by Eduardo Manet trans. Robert Baldick	25s	10s
PS 44	THE SLEEPERS DEN and OVER GARDENS OUT by Peter Gill	25s	10s
PS 45	A MACBETH by Charles Marowitz	30s	12s
PS 46	SLEUTH by Anthony Shaffer	25s	12s
*PS 47	SAMSON and ALISON MARY FAGAN by David Selbourne	25s	12s
*PS 48	OPERETTA by Witold Gombrowicz trans. Louis Iribarne	30s	12s
*PS 49	THE NUTTERS and other plays (Social Service, A Cure for Souls) by A.F. Cotterell	30s	12s
PS 50	THE GYMNASIUM and other plays (The Technicians, Stay Where You Are, Jack the Giant-Killer) by Olwen Wymark	30s	15s
PS 51	THE MAN IN THE GREEN MUFFLER and other plays (In Transit, The Sword) by Stewart Conn	25s	12s

		Cloth	Paper
*PS 52	CALCIUM and other plays (Coins, Broken, Victims, The Good Shine) by Jan Quackenbush	25s	12s
*PS 53	FOUR BLACK REVOLUTIONARY PLAYS (Experimental Death Unit 1, A Black Mass, Great Goodness of Life, Madheart) by Leroi Jones	25s	12s
PS 54	LONG VOYAGE OUT OF WAR by Ian Curteis	45s	21s
PS 55	INUIT and THE OTHERS by David Mowat	25s	12s
PS 57	CURTAINS by Tom Mallin	30s	12s
PS 58	VAGINA REX AND THE GAS OVEN by Jane Arden	25s	10s

*All plays marked thus are represented for dramatic
presentation by:
C and B (Theatre) Ltd, 18 Brewer Street London W1